It's Your Turn to Take Out the Trash

Getting the Garbage Out of Your Relationship

Abbi Hattem Ph.D.

Table of Contents

Acknowledgments

None of the people used to exemplify various concepts and self-help techniques are real. They are rather created from my own personal and professional experiences. When any one of them began to resemble a client with whom I've worked, I modified information to create more dissimilarity. Names and personal information are entirely fabricated.

The original manuscript was written over a period of time. I would like to thank my friends and family who offered encouragement and feedback on previous drafts.

Introduction

Chloe: You say you're happy to run errands, and then you come home with only about half the things on the list. Are you trying to aggravate me?

Alex: No, Chloe. The problem is, you're never satisfied with what I do for you.

or

Matt: Maybe if you weren't always talking on the phone, you'd be able to concentrate on what you're doing. You can't even boil an egg without burning it.

Zoë: It's called multi-tasking, but you don't understand that concept. And you don't get that if I got some help around here I wouldn't have to multi-task so much.

Sound familiar? And are you as tired of being chronically angry at your partner as Chloe, Alex, Matt, and Zoë are? Or are you a therapist, wondering whether their interest in continuing this argument is more powerful than your repertoire of interventions?

This book is about couples and their conflicts. We don't deal well with the concept of anger in our society, and many people are uncomfortable using the words conflict and fight. The terms frustration, aggravation, disagreements, and argument seem far more palatable to most people, although for some even those terms can be frightening.

Fight, especially, seems to mean scary, out-of-control anger. Even some schools of therapy recommend not allowing clients to argue during sessions, although I think it's important to get a sense of what goes on at home by seeing it, at least once, in the office. People say they would never fight or would do anything to avoid conflict. I think they mean they would not want to get angry and lose control. And a wise therapist will stop an argument before it spirals out of control.

Despite our cultural discomfort, I'm going to use the word fight. By fight, I mean what many people think of when they say disagree or argue. I certainly don't mean out of control. Nor, do I think violence has any place in any relationship. Rather, I think the word fight conveys the sense of the urgency and importance of the issues over which couples repeatedly disagree or argue.

We all discuss, debate, and sometimes even argue about fairly trivial matters, like what lunacy the school board or town council is up to. However important these issues are, they do not generate the same level of emotionality as disrespect or irresponsibility on the part of a life partner.

So, again, I am using the word fight to underscore the importance of the issues couples find difficult to resolve. The meaning of these issues, not the content of a particular argument, creates a sense of distress, frustration, and sometimes even hopelessness about the relationship.

The idea that all couples have one or two issues underlying all their fights occurred to me a number of years ago. At the time, I was working with two couples, each of whom could fight over anything.

Tim: It's so smoggy today the sky looks white.

Martha: No, it's light blue because of the haze.

One of the couples had been married many years, yet both spouses were able to recall the details of every fight they'd ever had. None of these fights had been resolved and so none of these fights had really ended; and their marriage had become a continuous struggle to resolve issues each considered important. The second couple had been married only a few years, but was equally adept at disagreeing about everything and never forgetting any of it.

These two husband-and-wife teams were the best fighters I'd ever seen, and working with them at the same time was enormously instructive. As I discovered I could not compete with the strength of their anger at one another, I began to ignore it and instead listen for what the rage was really about. One day, I said to one of these couples, "This is *the* fight again, isn't it." Although far more therapeutically brilliant words had come out of my mouth, this statement stopped the argument in its tracks. Both husband and wife agreed that yes, in fact this was *the* same old fight. After that, we focused on *the* fight, rather than on any particular argument or disagreement. The couple was then able to focus on their incompatibility and how to live with it, rather than on continuing efforts to convince the other to be someone s/he was not.

Since then, I have often referred to *the* fight in working with couples. While the concept is not magical, it helps to focus treatment on the issues that are important to the couple. I am hopeful that learning to recognize and resolve *the* fight in your relationship will help you, also.

It was several years later when I began to view *the* fight as a source of relationship garbage. The couple who led me to this insight was fighting over the division of labor in all aspects of their lives. They had been married long enough that the newness of their relationship had worn off. Disillusionment had begun to replace delight in one another, and the wife was starting to rethink the role she wished to play in the marriage. She described overflowing trashcans that he had promised to empty with sadness and anger. He became defensive, and they argued about how little time each had for housework and whose responsibility it really was.

The fight in their relationship was not about emptying the trashcans. Rather, it was about respect. When she looked at those trashcans, she saw not only that they were full, but also a husband who viewed her as the maid. But because this couple's arguments about housework had never touched on the issue of respect, neither the arguments nor *the* fight about respect was ever resolved. These ongoing arguments and the failure to resolve *the* fight thus became sources of relationship garbage.

I then began to think of garbage as metaphorical for the residue of *the* fight when it remains unresolved. *The* fight itself is about an issue that is critically important to both partners. If it did not matter much, one would yield and there would be resolution. In fact, the issue underlying *the* fight is so important that people are not only willing to fight over trivia as though defending their lives, but also to take time out of busy schedules and spend hard-earned money to share absurd scenarios with a virtual stranger in order to get help resolving the issue.

Unresolved fights lead to an accumulation of garbage in relationships. Every time a couple fights without addressing the underlying issue, it remains unresolved. Garbage results from both an accumulation of negative feelings from stirring up memories of previously unresolved arguments and frustration about the couple's current inability to resolve *the* fight.

The couple then must manage their frustration about their inability to resolve the issue, as well as the disagreement and their accumulated anger from past disagreements about the same issue.

Inevitably, subsequent arguments will remind them of all three sources of distress. And so, the relationship garbage piles higher.

When the issue itself can be identified and resolved, then a couple can learn to stop and resolve *the* fight. As a result, the garbage will begin to disappear. The couple is then left with only the disagreement, which is relatively easy to negotiate. For example, if the wife feels respected, the couple can negotiate emptying those pesky trashcans. A couple who is able to resolve their issues as they arise will generate almost no new garbage, and any garbage that is produced during their disagreements will decompose fast enough to be absorbed into the relationship.

This book is about a three-tiered model to identify and transform relationship distress. The first tier is the trash, or the content of the arguments and disagreements. It is the battleground for the second tier of the model, the underlying issue. *The* fight is always about this underlying issue. The third tier of the model is the relationship garbage, the residue of a couple's efforts to resolve *the* fight. It is *this* relationship garbage that couples need to get rid of before they become buried in it.

All relationships have trash. There is absolutely no way to live with another human being without becoming frustrated and angry on occasion. Even roommates fight. When the relationship is intimate and there is an expectation of permanence, the stakes become even higher and many more issues and situations become important.

Patrick complained that, although he's happy to start dinner since he usually gets home earlier than Beth, he resents having to clean up her breakfast dishes first. He thought asking Beth to clean up after herself would have been condescending but one evening when he was particularly tired, he yelled at her about his frustration with coming home to her dirty breakfast dishes and accused her of being inconsiderate.

Beth was appalled that he was so upset about such trivia and suggested he leave the dishes and simply start cooking. However reasonable her suggestion, it did not address Patrick feeling disrespected and taken for granted in the relationship. The dirty dishes were just one of many examples he could cite of Beth's lack of concern for his feelings and preferences.

The dirty dishes provided trash for their arguments. *The* fight was about whether Beth respected Patrick or took him for granted and emerged whether they were arguing about breakfast dishes, Beth making social plans without consulting him, or how she growls at him in the morning.

Every time Patrick and Beth fought about the trash (dirty dishes, social plans, morning grumpiness) instead of the issue (disrespect, being taken for granted), *the* fight remained unresolved. Patrick continued to feel disrespected and taken for granted, as well as frustrated by the dirty dishes, etc. Accumulation of ill will from unresolved fights about the trash, as well as prolonged hurt and anger around the unresolved issue, became the garbage in Patrick and Beth's relationship.

Again, it is this relationship garbage that couples need to get rid of before they become buried in it. The first step to getting rid of the garbage involves identifying *the* fight, as distinct from the trash. You cannot stop *the* fight until you recognize it. The second step is resolving *the* fight. Then, you can begin putting aside the garbage, or accumulated ill-will. Think of this phase of your task as taking your relationship garbage to the street and waving happily as someone carries it to the dump, where it belongs.

In Part 1, I will talk more about the concepts of trash, *the* fight, and relationship garbage and illustrate them with stories about couples. Nine issues that frequently underlie the fight will be discussed, with examples, to help you identify and resolve the issue in your own relationship fight in Parts 2 and 3.

In Part 2, I will provide you with a method for identifying your own fight or helping the couples you see in therapy to identify theirs. The goal will be to increase your awareness of *the* fight, your own and your partner's reactions to it, and to recognizing how your reactions to one another and your attempts to resolve *the* fight in your relationship may be creating garbage. I will use the couples' stories from Part 1 to illustrate how to identify *the* fight or sometimes fights in your relationship.

Finally, in Part 3, I will describe tools and techniques you can use to transform your awareness into options for resolving *the* fight and getting rid of the garbage. I will again use the same couples' stories to illustrate these techniques.

Therapists using this book will need to step back from the personal experience requested of couples using it as a self-help book. Instead, therapists can use the concepts and techniques, as well as empathy, to help the couples they see increase their awareness and identify and enact options for change. As always, it is crucial to be able to take the perspective of each partner and the role of their interactions in their relationship, rather than falling into the trap of seeing one as valid and the other as difficult.

All of the individuals and couples used as examples throughout this book are fictional and not intended to represent any individual or couple with whom I have worked. However, they have grown out of my experience, both personal and professional, and are intended to exemplify realistic scenarios and dialogue. When they have sounded very reminiscent of a particular client with whom I've worked, I have changed the scenario and dialogue to create a composite of several situations. Thus, if you can identify yourself or someone you know, such recognition is a statement of a basic fact of our humanity: that we are all more similar than different.

Part I
Relationship Garbage

1

What Is Relationship Garbage?

Have you ever wished you could gather up all the negative feelings and repetitive fights in your relationship—like the Lego pieces strewn around a household with young children—pile them into a trash can, haul them to the sidewalk, and be rid of them forever? Have you ever picked up your partner's socks or wet towel and wanted to scream? Or, has your partner ever been late and you've fantasized a horrible car wreck—and not been all that upset?

Living closely with another person is difficult and provides numerous opportunities for annoyance and misunderstanding. These annoyances and misunderstandings comprise the trash in a relationship, the content of couple fights, arguments, disagreements, debates, or whatever word you would like to use to define your own experience with your partner. Using the trash metaphor, every relationship has the kind of trash you find in wastebaskets in the various rooms of your home.

The trash itself is probably pretty boring: orange peels, rotten lettuce leaves, tissues, and junk mail that didn't get recycled. Occasionally, it's beer cans on the front lawn, but mostly blues songs symbolize everyday experience by embellishing it (1).

Most couples have some rules to determine who empties the trash, when s/he does it, how often s/he does it, and the consequences of not doing it. I find couples' rules fascinating. Why? Because rules are very revealing about people's expectations, and thus about their distress.

For some couples, it's the man's job to take out the trash. Is this so because bagging the trash and hauling it to the street is a traditionally masculine job? Does he have a more leisurely start on the day trash is collected? Or, was taking out the trash one of his chores growing up? If so, did he like it, learn to tolerate it, assume he'd always be the one to do it, or figure out ways to avoid his obligation? As you can imagine, if he spent his childhood devising ways to avoid taking out the trash, he will be quite skilled at evading the task by the time he reaches adulthood and finds himself in a committed relationship. And, his partner may become increasingly frustrated about his not taking out the trash, or even interpret his behavior as irresponsible and childish or inconsiderate and uncaring.

> Barbara: He can't remember to take out the trash, even when I remind him. Sometimes I feel like he's like a little boy trying to put one over on his mommy.

> Jim: I resent that, Barb. And, it's not even true.

For other couples, the woman takes out the trash. Is this because the couple values alternative gender roles, or because she has given up that her partner will ever take out the trash? Has she bartered being financially supported for full responsibility for the house? Or, did her older brother take out the trash while she was growing up and because he seemed grown up and competent, she values doing what he did?

Still other couples share the job. Some couples have elaborate schemes whereby jobs are divvied up equitably, sometimes by interest, sometimes by availability, and sometimes each job is rotated on a weekly or monthly basis. Such schemes often reflect a couple's desire to mutually respect one another, by maintaining a sense of fairness between them.

Finally, there are couples in which one or both partners empty the trash as needed during the week, and then one is designated to haul the cans to the street before pick up time. This is often a good solution when a messy house disturbs one partner more than the other. The one who prefers neatness is often more motivated to monitor the flow of trash from the containers to the larger cans outside the home.

These distinctions may sound trivial. However, they are immensely important. They variously reflect shared values, marital distress, preferences, and both personal and shared histories. The man who takes out the trash because he leaves later on collection day and the woman who takes out the trash because the couple values alternative gender roles are acting out of shared values about delegation of tasks. On the other hand, the woman who is frustrated by her partner's ability to avoid doing his chores is expressing the couple's distress. The woman who respected her older brother and the man who became a skilled avoider are enacting their personal histories. Finally, the woman who has bartered financial security for housework, as well as delegation of the one who prefers neatness to monitor the trash, are reflections of the role of couple history in assigning chores.

The most fascinating thing about couple rules, whether about trash or anything else, is what happens when they're violated. If it's your turn to take out the trash and you don't do it, for whatever good or not-so-great reason, then what happens?

There are usually two types of consequences of breaking a relationship rule. The first is fairly straight-forward: the trash piles up, the house smells, the cans are full before the next pick-up day, and, eventually, the health department condemns your home. The partner who forgot or neglected to do the job has to do it next week or pay a fine to a jar which, when full, is used to do something fun together. Even being yelled at for not taking out the trash is a straightforward consequence. These are the *overt* consequences of breaking a relationship rule; whatever these consequences are, they are not a surprise.

The second type of consequence of breaking a rule is less apparent. It's the *covert* consequence. This is often the emotional consequence of breaking a couple's rule. By observing the reaction of the partner who did not break the rule, one can identify the covert consequences of violating it.

When a partner can be relied upon to do his or her chores most of the time, the covert consequences of failing to take out the trash may be minimal, even compassionate. For example, "Oh well, these things happen." Notice that the speaker assumes the partner did not forget the trash intentionally or in order to infuriate. S/he gave the benefit of the doubt to her/his partner.

However, if one partner consistently fails to live by the couple rules, then anger, resentment, accusations, and a sense of betrayal or disrespect may result. The covert consequence of not taking out the trash becomes evidence of the forgetful person's lack of caring, interest, or respect or how unimportant the partner is to her/him.

> Sharon: Jeff remembers important things, like who he's having lunch with today.

While it's easy to hear the anger in Sharon's statement, she is also expressing a lot of pain about feeling unimportant to Jeff, the person who promised Sharon she would always be important to him. Jeff, however, is more likely to hear and respond to Sharon's anger than her pain.

> Jeff: What am I supposed to say to that?

And Sharon will then hear Jeff's frustration, rather than any sort of assurance of her importance to him. Most likely, his frustration will fuel her upset.

If one partner forgot to take out the trash, the other may hurl accusations of laziness, passive-aggression, or being taken for granted. S/he may be resentful, or even martyred:

Julie [condescending]: That's OK, Honey; I know you have more important things to do.

Yeah, right, she may think, like channel surfing. She may feel betrayed, because the trash is only one of many examples she can cite of his broken promises, lack of reliability, or values she cannot reconcile with her own.

Trust and shared values are critical to most people's views of being a couple. The absence of either usually results in distress. Partners often attempt to convince one another to be "more like me", and sometimes these efforts manifest in verbal attacks. In the blues song quoted at the beginning of Part 1, the comment about beer cans on the lawn represents the woman's anger that her man is neither working nor cleaning up after himself. The singer, voicing the feelings of many women, is burdened by the work of compensating for his broken promises of sharing responsibility.

Here's where the trash is no longer contained in wastebaskets. Rather, it overflows, turning into *the* couple fight. The issue in *the* fight is no longer the trash itself. The issue is now some variant of, "Can I count on you?" "Do you promise whatever you think will appease me, without ever intending to follow through?" "Do you take for granted that I will clean up after whatever mess you make?" "Do you respect me at all?" "Why are you with me—for a maid service?"

Julie [to therapist]: It's so embarrassing. The house starts smelling and I say, "George, don't you think it's time to take the trash out?" And he sits there reading the paper, saying, "I'll get to it later" like it's no big deal.

George: Yeah, and I will.

Julie: When? When do you ever "get to it"?

George: Hey. If I want to take a few minutes to unwind, I have that right. [To therapist] She exaggerates; the trash doesn't really smell.

Therapist: Really?

George: Well, I can't smell it.

Julie [furious]: Unwind? Do you see me having time to unwind? I've been at work all day, too, and then I've picked up the kids. And then you expect me to work some more, cooking dinner and cleaning up in a disgusting house while you're "unwinding"?

She might as well have said, "I need some respect for how hard I work, too." And George may, in fact, have been able to give her respect for how hard she works had she asked for it directly and without reference to the trash. But by this point in the argument, George and Julie were so far into protecting themselves from the other's accusations that the issue of respect was overlooked.

It is clear from the following that George realized the argument was escalating. While he attempted to appease Julie, he failed because he did not address what was really bothering her: the feeling that he does not respect her.

George [appeasing]: Honey, look, it's only trash. So what if I don't always remember to take it out? The trash collectors will be here next week—same time, same day. I don't know why we're wasting therapy time talking about this.

Julie [still furious]: Don't condescend to me, you sanctimonious….

Therapist: I'm going to stop you here, Julie. Tell me what would have happened at home, where I wouldn't have been able to interrupt you?

Julie: [softer voice] I would have called him a jerk and he would have refused to talk anymore. [Sighs] And then I would have made dinner.

The issue of respect is far more important than an overflowing trash can, even if the trashcan smells bad. But since the issue of respect was masked by the trash and the anger, it was neither addressed nor resolved. *The* fight about respect will continue for Julie and George, and their anger from all their unresolved arguments about respect, like the one above, will continue to add to it and thus become relationship garbage.

In this example, Julie felt disrespected and frustrated, and George neither heard nor responded to her plea for respect. At the same time, George felt hurt and angry about Julie's criticism of his behavior, her name-calling, and perhaps even the implication that he's not a good partner. Unfortunately, he can easily tell himself Julie is unreasonable, unkind, and disrespectful to him, because he knows good partners don't always prioritize chores. They do, however, display respect. So, when chores become entangled with respect, the potential for miscommunication and unresolved arguments is enormous.

The problem with relationship garbage is that one never knows when anything, from a rotting lettuce leaf to an extramarital affair, will stir it up. Even arguments unrelated to *the* fight become huge, because they can elicit the garbage independently of *the* fight. For Julie and George, frustration with themselves and each other about repeated failures to resolve their disputes can make either or both angry. And the anger then calls forth the feeling of disrespect, generating even more anger.

On the surface, the upset partner may look pretty ridiculous. How much upset is really warranted by overflowing wastebaskets, or even the smell of decomposing vegetables? But when those overflowing wastebaskets represent an overflow of stored disappointment and hurt, they become far more important, and the upset becomes far more understandable and not at all ridiculous, as George and Julie's fight demonstrates.

A single event, such as an extra-marital affair, may create a sudden crisis in a relationship. In the absence of such a precipitating event, most couples accumulate their garbage gradually. The little fights, which are rampant in the first couple of years of cohabiting, may never get resolved. Or, one partner may feel so wounded or unable to defend her/himself in these squabbles that their impact long outlives the arguments themselves. Then, any subsequent disagreement occurs against the backdrop of hurt, anger, helplessness, and previously unresolved conflict. The backdrop, or garbage, which is not addressed in the new argument, makes a positive resolution of the new tension less likely, and so the hurt, anger, helplessness, and negative feelings grow. Ten or twenty years of this are hard on the individuals and on their relationship. Years of disagreements that overlook *the* fight and thus don't get resolved may undermine any hope the partners have that their interactions can be different.

No one goes to a couples' therapist for help dividing the job of emptying wastebaskets. Couple therapy, not being a whole lot of fun and frequently not covered by insurance, is usually initiated only when the garbage, as opposed to the trash, has become overwhelming. Even when the words sound like the subject is trash, trash alone is simply not important enough to take to a therapist. And, the same can be said of divorce. The trash that is brought to a therapist or an attorney always represents a lack of resolution of an important couple issue and the subsequent accumulation of garbage that is burying the relationship.

The point of this book is to help you identify an accumulation of garbage in your relationship, hopefully before it overwhelms the bond between you and your partner, and resolve *the* fight that precipitated the accumulation of your garbage. Then, the flow of trash in and out of your relationship can be similar to the flow of trash in and out of your kitchen. When it's gone, it's gone, even though you can expect more. Some weeks there's less trash than others, and most of the time it's a part of the landscape you mostly ignore.

Fritz Perls, founder of gestalt therapy, called his autobiography In and Out of the Garbage Pail (2). If we could all apprehend the real issues and address them effectively, we would circumvent much of our unhappiness. But the real issues are masked by trivia, or trash. And without an awareness of what is really the matter, or an ability to sift through the trash for the real issues, there is little hope of stopping the build-up of garbage. For many couples, this means that garbage eventually destroys what was initially a loving relationship.

It's important that my use of the term relationship garbage does not trivialize the seriousness of its impact. The fact that two people who deeply care for and respect each other and who have made a commitment to a life-long relationship grow to disrespect and even despise each other is tragic. The concept of *the* fight is a way to distinguish the important issues in a relationship from the apparent trivia (trash) in which they are frequently disguised, and from the ill will (garbage) which accumulates when these issues remain unresolved.

Everyone knows that babies need a strong, emotional attachment to at least one dependable adult in order to survive and grow. Lack of such an attachment has been associated with all sorts of horrible outcomes, including personality disorders and depression, delayed physical and cognitive growth, and even death (3).

Adults also need a strong, emotional attachment to another dependable adult. While our survival may not hinge on it, our emotional and physical wellbeing does (4). When such an attachment is threatened, our sense of self, our confidence in our choices, and our certainty that we have the ability to feel close to other people are all also threatened. Even the delight we experience in life may fade when we live in a chronically distressed relationship.

External factors, such as illness or job loss, can neither be predicted nor controlled. So, my focus will be on the difficulties that are internal to the relationship. When couples identify and resolve important issues in ways that avoid an accumulation of garbage, they are better able to deal with whatever problems arise.

2

The Couple Fight

Every couple develops one or more themes that underlie all their fights. These themes represent personal differences, interpersonal misunderstandings, and cultural myths and demands. You'll notice these when you tell yourself you or someone else "should" behave, think, or feel a certain way.

The themes of a couple's fights are usually metaphors for the unresolved issues in their relationship. Most couples recognize that *the* fight exists, although they usually are unable to describe how it developed or recognize when it occurs. For example, a couple may fight about keeping the house clean, whether both will continue working after a child is born, or planning and enforcing homework or chores schedules for the children. All these fights may share a common theme, for example, respect or trust.

I am going to describe nine themes of couple fights gleaned from my experience doing therapy with couples. These nine themes, or issues, appeared regularly, whether the year was 1985 or 2010; a couple was married or cohabiting; straight, gay, or lesbian; divorced and attempting to deal with continued co-parenting; or re-married and attempting to deal with one another's children and spouses from previous marriages.

These nine themes are not intended to be exhaustive. If there is a repetitive fight in your relationship that doesn't fall into one of these categories, please keep reading. You may learn something helpful from someone else's experience and working through the exercises in Parts 2 and 3 doesn't depend on your fight fitting one of these categories.

The nine themes are:

- *Respect and Importance*
- *Caring*
- *Trust*
- *Loyalty*
- *Intimacy*
- *Shared Values*
- *Boundaries & Distance Regulation*
- *Relationship Contract*
- *Power*

I will address each of these themes separately, although in most relationships two or more themes may be present in *the* fight. This complexity will be illustrated in Chapter 3, where I describe four couples' stories in detail. In the examples in this chapter, I will intentionally simplify couples' situations, to more clearly demonstrate the nine themes.

Respect and Importance

People don't spend a lot of time talking about how much they respect their partners. Most people assume mutual respect exists, until one or both partners sense its absence.

The absence of respect shows up in a lot of ways. When one's voice tone contains exasperation, condescension, or sneering, one's partner knows s/he is not being viewed with respect.

Another way of communicating lack of respect is through compliments or displays of empathy that, in context, are really put-downs. "You've got the cleanest house in the neighborhood" may sound like a compliment, until dialogue is filled in around it:

Pam: You take your socks off and toss them on the floor wherever you are, like I'm the maid, just dying for something else to do.

Bob: I get really tired of you picking at me for every little thing. I can't do anything right.

Pam: You could try caring about how our home looks.

Bob : You care enough for both of us. You've got the cleanest house in the neighborhood. [sarcastic] Perfect Pam needs a perfect house and a perfect husband to put inside it.

His unstated message? You care more about how the house looks than about me, and I don't respect you for prioritizing how things look over who I am.

Similarly, "He's always a nervous wreck" may sound empathetic. But listen to these two contexts in which one partner describes the other.

Tina: I'm really worried about him. He's always a nervous wreck. Men his age have blood pressure problems and heart attacks when they're wound this tightly. But he won't listen to me when I suggest going to the doctor.

Tina's voice tone is consistent with her verbal message: I'm worried about him, and I can't think of what else to do.

Teresa: He's always a nervous wreck. He worries about everything. We'll be lying in bed, and he'll ask me, "Did you pay that bill that came in the mail yesterday? Did you turn off the light in the kitchen?" He starts this even when I'm almost asleep. And he won't stop until *I*—not him—have gotten up and checked the lights and the locks.

Whether her voice tone conveys humor or exasperation, Teresa's words contain no empathy or respect for him. Rather, her message conveys her belief that he worries excessively and places his own comfort above consideration for her need to sleep.

Body language is also a subtle way people communicate lack of respect for one another. A woman who sits next to her partner, lifts her shoulder, and angles her back a few degrees so he is looking at her shoulder blade may be saying, "It makes me sick to look at you." A man who picks up the newspaper while his partner talks to him may as well say, "I refuse to waste my time listening to you."

When partners stop feeling respected by one another, the relationship may seem pretty hopeless. Respect is a form of liking, and when people no longer like one another, they find the daily difficulties of living intimately almost impossible.

The good news, however, is that partners can stop feeling respected by one another without actually losing respect for one another. In the absence of respectful statements or when words conflict with behavior, each partner assumes respect or lack thereof from the other's actions. And, when the house is strewn with trash, it becomes easy to misinterpret one's partner's conduct as evidence of something it's not.

Melissa and Paul were so busy raising their four children that they rarely found time to talk about anything else. Although they had decided that having Melissa at home would be better for them financially than paying for child care while she worked outside the home, they had not talked about how Melissa would maintain a sense of herself in the face of family demands. So, as the children got older and Melissa began to miss the challenge of her former work, it became easy for her to interpret Paul's apparent lack of communication about anything besides the children as a sign that he'd lost respect for her intelligence.

When Melissa finally verbalized her concern, Paul was very convincing in his response. He talked about how much he respected Melissa's mothering and homemaking skills, citing successes and happy memories that he attributed to Melissa's work for the family. And Melissa responded, telling him how important it was for her to hear that he still respected her, especially at times when she felt she was losing herself. They went on to discuss how Melissa might begin to return to the career she enjoyed.

But, even when partners have lost respect for one another, the loss is not always irreparable. For example, a woman whose respect for her partner has diminished as he's prioritized work over time with the family may regain respect for him when he either reassesses his life goals or explains them to her.

Feeling important to one's partner is closely linked to feeling respected. No one feels important without feeling respected. For example, when a woman believes her partner respects the hard work she does in her profession, she is less likely to view the time he spends away from her as a sign that she is not important to him than she would if she felt he did not respect her work. Conversely, if he frequently complains about her disorganization, the state of the house, or how the children are behaving, she may conclude that he doesn't respect her. Then, when he becomes busy at work, she is more likely to interpret his busyness as another symptom of her lack of importance to him. For example, "If I mattered to you, you'd want to spend more time with me."

People perceive that they are unimportant to their partners by observing the partner's behavior. While respect can be communicated verbally and nonverbally, importance is usually only communicated nonverbally.

Nor is a sense of unimportance the result of a single event.

Alexia: I know I'm important to him—after his work, golf, his car, the dog, and the kids.

This is the kind of statement that follows lengthy experience observing his priorities in action. How many events that were important to her or the kids did he bow out of at the last minute because he "had" to work? How often did he make golf plans without checking whether the kids had activities that morning or she needed time to clean house and cook for guests? Did he agree to help the children with their homework and then change his clothes and go work on the car right after dinner? Or volunteer for yet another evening meeting? Does he always play with the dog when he arrives home and rarely greet Alexia?

All of these behaviors can be messages that he's angry. But, in the absence of loud fighting, she will more likely interpret them as evidence that she is unimportant to him.

Once we have drawn a conclusion about our situation, it becomes a belief against which we interpret future experience. A woman who feels she is unimportant to her partner may also conclude, from the same evidence, that he takes her for granted. And who respects someone they take for granted?

How do respect and importance become *the* fight in a relationship? First, one partner notices s/he doesn't feel respected and/or important to the other. Then, the wish to be respected and feel important begins to underlie arguments about anything and everything. A disagreement about whose turn is it to wash the dog easily becomes a fight about whether one avoids chores as a sign of disrespect for the other's time or of taking the other for granted.

The fight becomes: "If I were important to you, or if you respected me, then you would want to do more around the house so I wouldn't feel so burdened and you would want to spend more time with me." When this sentence remains unspoken, *the* fight cannot be resolved. And so it continues, about the dog, the dishes, what time each comes home, what plans who makes without consulting the other, etc.

Partners tend to defend against an implied accusation, even if the core of *the* fight is never stated. "You don't do enough around here or get home when you say you will or consult me about anything" is an attack. Few people want to view themselves as unhelpful, unfair, or uncaring. So, to protect his self-esteem from the assault, the accused is likely to either attack the accuser to prove she's no better, deny the accusation even if it derives from serious pain, or invalidate the accuser. "You were late last year," "I wash the dishes whenever you leave them stacked in the sink all night," and "You've planned vacations without asking for my input" are all ways of saying, "You're no better than I am so stop accusing me." "Am not," "Are, too" are also ways of refuting an accusation. Either tack can easily increase ill will in the relationship. And neither tack addresses the issue so neither allows it to be resolved.

Most defensive responses fail to address the accusation, leaving the accuser feeling unheard and therefore even more disrespected, uncared about, and upset. "You were late last year" doesn't begin to address the pain of one's partner forgetting an important occasion. And when the accuser adds not being heard to the list of grievances, a couple takes yet another step away from addressing *the* fight about respect and importance while adding to garbage.

Both partners elicit empathy in such situations. It's awful to attempt to communicate an important and probably painful feeling to an important person and feel that both the message and the pain were ignored. Similarly, the frustration and defensiveness of the accused partner clearly stem from upset about her/his partner's unhappiness and anger, as well as hurt for being blamed. The need to be respected and feel important and the hurt at its perceived absence become obscured in defensiveness and anger.

As the garbage accumulates, partners may ask themselves, why risk expressing pain if the result is only more pain? And why bother to do anything for someone who instead of being appreciative will accuse me of not doing it right? Anger and hurt feelings become garbage. They are easily accessed in future arguments and incarnations of *the* fight, leading at some point to a sense of futility about the relationship.

Caring

Caring is a word with many meanings. Caring about someone means devoting time, energy, and emotion to her/him. However, the details of such devotion vary. For some people, caring about a partner means spending time together. For others, it means taking the partner's reaction into consideration in all things. For still others, caring involves attempting to make life better for the other person. And for yet others, honoring vows of monogamy and financial support denote caring.

How partners express caring for one another is usually part of their unspoken relationship contract. At this point, I would like to talk about caring itself, and the myriad opportunities that exist to misinterpret disagreements about how to express caring as signs that the other doesn't really care at all. I will talk about relationship contracts later in this chapter.

Most people assume two people in love define caring in the same way and thus do for their partner what they want her/him to do for them. Unfortunately, the partner may want something entirely different. When Lucy is not feeling well, she likes to go to bed with a cup of hot tea and be left alone to recover. But Phil likes to be pampered when he is not feeling well. He wants Lucy to bring him meals on a tray and sit with him while he eats, and to call from her office during the day to ask him how he's feeling. Lucy complains that Phil is disrespectful of her needs, inconsiderate, and uncaring when he refuses to leave her alone when she's sick. And, Phil is equally hurt by what he views as Lucy's insensitivity when he is unwell and she virtually ignores him.

Similar issues about caring arise for couples around holidays and birthday celebrations. In Olivia's family, birthdays were occasions of great excitement and attention. The birthday celebrant selected menus for all three meals and the type of cake her mother prepared. There were calls from extended family members who didn't live nearby, cupcakes sent to school, and balloons tied to her chair at the table. Presents were given, and Olivia remembers having a birthday party with friends every year. Her mother's siblings who lived nearby got together every month or two to celebrate family birthdays.

Pete grew up in a family where birthdays were inconsequential events. His mother didn't bake, and the only birthday party he remembers was one when he was very small. He would always receive a birthday gift, but without much fuss. He did not remember his parents celebrating their birthdays.

When Olivia and Pete were married, Olivia collected the birth dates of his friends and family and sent cards every year. After they became parents, Pete deferred to Olivia. He didn't help plan their children's birthday celebrations, but he didn't resist them either. Olivia expressed concern that his lack of enthusiasm might detract from their children's enjoyment.

After years of having her own birthday ignored by Pete and his family, and of being solely responsible for family celebrations, Olivia began to feel taken for granted. She interpreted Pete's failure to remember her birthday as a sign that he didn't care about her.

Olivia found the notion that one could forget the birthday of someone he cared about inconceivable. Conversely, Pete couldn't comprehend that an event as insignificant as a birthday could generate so much upset in Olivia. Their incredulity about each other's attitudes distracted them from seeing that caring, rather than birthdays, was the theme of *the* fight in their relationship. And failure to address the theme led to lack of resolution to *the* fight.

Olivia: If you cared about me, you'd remember my birthday.

Pete: What? You can't be serious.

Olivia: Oh, I'm dead serious. You can trivialize this, Pete, but that only makes me angrier.

Pete: No, seriously. You claim I don't care about you, and all you can come up with, as an example, is that I don't run to the Hallmark store every year and buy you a birthday card?

Olivia: Or a mother's day card or an anniversary card….

Therapist: Pete, how did your father remember your mother's birthday?

Pete: He didn't. I guess sometimes they went out to dinner, but I think that was for their anniversary. I don't know. I don't remember.

Olivia: That's awful.

Therapist: Well, it's different than what you grew up with. And this difference seems to be one you both have difficulty understanding.

Later in the conversation, the therapist will speculate about what would happen if Olivia interpreted Pete ignoring occasions and Pete interpreted Olivia's celebrations as nothing more than differences in how they learned to observe occasions.

A more complicated interpretation of caring arises when one or both partners expects one to take care of the other. This can result in resentment by one or both that s/he is either being parented by or parenting another adult. For example, worrying about what the other eats or protecting the other from the consequences of her or his forgetfulness may feel to the worrier/protector like parenting and like being parented to the one worried about or protected.

In the extreme, this is the codependency of protecting a partner from the consequences of her or his abusive behavior. Whether one is protecting one's partner from the consequences of substance abuse, or from something milder, like forgetfulness, being protected prevents that partner from changing.

Some people expect one partner to be the other's caretaker. This becomes a set-up for each to feel that there is nothing left over for her/him. If one partner is considered too inept to cook dinner, then the other has to be home every night at dinnertime, despite other commitments or wishes.

> Molly: I can't come to your book group. Lou can't even put a frozen leftover in the microwave.

Instead of feeling cared about, the protected partner may feel resentful, confusing the protector, who equates protection with caring.

> Lou: I'm perfectly capable of making my own dinner. Or, I can go out. I wish you'd stop coming home to cook for me as though I'm a little boy when it's completely reasonable for you to be in a book group with your friends.

Resentment also arises in the protecting partner when the other seems ungrateful. Molly could interpret Lou's words as a lack of gratitude for the sacrifices she makes for him.

Finally, resentment may arise when one partner believes care taking is necessary to the functioning of the other and then labels the other immature for needing the care.

> Melissa: If I don't remind you, you don't do it.

Sam: So, if you want it done, you have to remind me.

Melissa: It's not my job to do your thinking for you.

Sam: I'm not asking you to think for me. I'm telling you: if it's important to you that I remember something, you need to remind me. Otherwise, I might forget.

Melissa: Well, I'm not your mother. Find a way to remind yourself.

Sam: You know, I'm sick of your condescension.

Caring about one's partner sometimes means prioritizing that person's needs. At the same time, we live in a culture where we are taught that attending to our own needs is selfish and bad. Often, no distinction is made between self-care and lack of concern and empathy for others. So, a woman who takes an hour or two for herself, a sacred time to regenerate, may consider herself or be considered selfish by others. She is treated, or may treat herself, as though she was unconcerned about the needs of her family, even when her children and partner are elsewhere. After all, she could be volunteering at her children's school, doing an errand, or cleaning house. Many women wind up feeling that taking an hour for themselves is equivalent to leaving a hurt child to cry because it's time for a manicure or telling a partner she could really care less about what an awful day he's had.

Cultural mythology holds that anything we could do for someone else and don't do, for any reason, is as bad as ignoring our commitments to them. This myth leaves us all vulnerable to feeling that if we care about our partner we will toss aside our own needs, wants, and other commitments at her or his slightest whim. When one says, "If you're going to the drugstore today, could you pick up my prescription?" the other may interpret the question as a demand. When "if it's convenient for you" always means "drop everything and do this for me no matter how trivial it seems or how much you wanted or needed to do something else," it doesn't take the one who feels compelled to comply long to feel resentful. And from resentment, it's a quick leap to interpreting the demand to mean lack of caring.

Sally: Do you ever think about me, about what I want? It's as though you think I have nothing to do all day long but run errands for you.

Sally sounds resentful, irrespective of whether her partner intended a demand or she misinterpreted the request as one. The only difference between hiding a demand behind a question and Sally misinterpreting a question as a demand is that being misinterpreted may confuse her partner.

When one partner believes the unrealistic expectation that caring means prioritizing the other's needs without considering one's own, the distinction between a demand and a request blurs, leaving room for *the* fight about caring to develop. It's often not our partner's expectation, but our own that leaves us unable to attend to our own needs and desires. And when one partner equates caring with not asking for anything, s/he is a short step away from blaming the other for wanting anything.

The question becomes, is one partner making demands, such as, "Pick up my dry cleaning today" or is s/he including the option for her/his partner to say no?

Rob: Do you have time to pick up my dry cleaning today?

Sally: [to therapist] If he cared about me, he wouldn't always be asking me to do this and that on my lunch hour.

Consider the alternative:

Rob: Do you have time to pick up my dry cleaning for me today?

Sally: Well, I was planning to walk with Patsy at lunch and then I need to get our son at soccer practice right after work. I could skip the walk.

Rob: No, it's not that important.

Rob's question may have the same meaning, as well as the same words, in both examples, but in the former Sally interprets it as a demand, perhaps because of her own beliefs about expressing caring or perhaps because it is a demand hidden by a question. In the second example, although she again prioritizes his need over hers, she allows him to clarify their relative importance.

When one partner views her/his own needs as secondary to the other's, the only way a couple can avoid requests turning into fights about caring is to agree that caring involves not asking for anything. If asking means not caring to Sally, then she and Rob must choose between self-reliance or failure to care. This choice may be confusing for Rob if he believes partnership involves mutuality, or interdependence. *The* fight arises when couples disagree about the line between a request and a demand, and a request then becomes a sign of not caring.

Here, again, caring and respect overlap. Just as one partner might interpret a demand as inconsiderate, s/he might also view repetitive demands as evidence her/his partner lacks respect for her/his time. Respect is a part of caring. But caring is also different from respect; it's possible to respect someone, for example, a colleague or a supervisor, without caring about that person. Partners are usually sensitive to a diminishment of either respect or caring in their relationship.

Jim: I think she's a wonderful person. She does a great job at work and with the kids. But, she's let herself go, she doesn't talk to me much. I don't think she even likes me. How am I supposed to want to rush home from work to be with her?

Jim's partner would probably hear nothing before the "but." In other words, she would quickly discern that Jim no longer cares to spend time with her. That he may continue to respect her professionally and as a parent of their children becomes meaningless by comparison.

I think the most insidious myth about caring involves mind reading. If you love me, you will know what I'm thinking and feeling. In reality, we can never entirely understand how someone else experiences the world because we cannot completely share her/his biology and history. In other words, it's impossible. Yet many people insist that if they have to ask, it means their partner doesn't care enough to figure it out.

One way this plays out is deciding where to eat when a couple goes out. One asks the other where s/he wants to go, and the response is, "I don't care. Whatever you want." But the partner suspects this is not entirely the case, or doesn't really care much either. Lengthy and repetitive arguments occur over the veracity of, "I don't care" and how much one has to care to name a restaurant. These arguments often arise from attempts to communicate care: if I choose a restaurant then I am being inconsiderate of your preferences, and I want to show you how much I care about you. Therefore, I don't care where we eat, how long it takes us to decide where to go, or how frustrated we become with one another during the decision-making process, for to name a restaurant would demonstrate that I don't care about you when in fact I do.

Another way to equate not asking for what one wants with caring involves the assumption that if the partner doesn't already know then s/he doesn't care.

Therapist: If you want a date night with him, why don't you suggest it?

Sally: It wouldn't mean anything if I had to ask.

Therapist: Really? Help me understand.

Sally: Well, if he wanted to go out with me, he'd ask. And he remembers how much I used to enjoy our date nights when we had them.

In a truly caring relationship, both one's own and one's partner's needs receive respect and are prioritized whenever possible. "Whenever possible" acknowledges that sometimes we must put ourselves first, even if it makes our partner unhappy, and sometimes we must put her or him first, even when we'd rather not.

Trust

Most people agree that trust is essential to any important relationship. Eric Erickson studied human development throughout the lifespan. He wrote that the major psychological task of the first six months of life is establishing basic trust. For a baby, adult responsiveness to cries of distress—hunger, pain, discomfort from a wet diaper, cold, wanting to be held—is critical to developing a sense of trust. When caretakers either ignore or become angry when the baby cries in distress, that baby is left with a sense that the world is not safe. Adults who were abused or neglected as infants or young children usually experience difficulty trusting others. So do adults who were separated from a parent due to illness or death when they were very young.

Adults also need to feel safe and loved, even though the fulfillment of those needs is not essential to survival, as it is for infants and children. Dr. Leslie Greenberg has developed a theory and counseling practice around the idea that adults, as well as children, need another adult to love and feel attached to. When trust has been established in a relationship and is then violated, this sense of being loved and attached is also threatened.

Trust in a relationship can be violated in several ways. The first, and most obvious, is an affair. Couples who are not married and who have agreed to be monogamous also violate trust when one or the other has sex outside the relationship.

A second, and related, violation of trust can occur when one or the other partner becomes involved in an intimate, nonsexual relationship outside their monogamous relationship. Lisa had never been threatened by Gary's friendships with women at work. Both agreed that he is more comfortable with women and would always have women friends. However, when he began to prioritize time with one of them over time with Lisa, she became suspicious, fearing the loss of his love and the weakening of their attachment. Apprehensive that he was having an affair, she started looking in his briefcase and through his computer files. When Gary discovered she had been reading his e-mails, he, too, became angry. He felt his privacy had been violated, and told Lisa her snooping had diminished his trust in her.

A less obvious violation of trust occurs when either partner feels s/he cannot count on the other to follow-through on promises. These promises can be extremely important, such as looking for a job or giving up smoking. Or, they can appear trivial and yet signify a gradual erosion of trust. Failing to take out the trash or to remember the bottle of milk s/he promised to pick up on the way home becomes extremely significant in an environment in which one partner is unable to feel confident the other will do what s/he promises. "You said you'd bring home the milk" or "How could you forget I bought tickets to that concert? You promised you'd be home in time to go" become indistinguishable from, "You said you'd never cheat on me" or "How could you love someone else more than you love me?"

Loyalty

Loyalty is a combination of attachment, trust, and importance. We all develop loyalties to individuals and groups. Whether it's a basketball team, a group at work, or a family, loyalty implies commitment, membership, caring, importance, and trust.

Couple loyalty implies a commitment to both the partner as a person and to the relationship as a unit. Often, loyalty also means defending the partner and the relationship from perceived threats, such as a critical in-law. However, partners may not agree about the nature of the perceived threat or the need to defend the other from it.

> Susan: You promised you'd say something to your mother the next time she criticized me for working [outside the home].
>
> David: You know how she is, Susan. If I thought it would do any good, believe me I'd say something.

Susan believed loyalty meant defending her whenever his mother criticized her. David, however, believed in limiting the expression of such loyalty to those times when the outcome might be affected. He believed that his mother would never accept the notion of women choosing to work outside the home. However, he did think that if he asked his mother to stop when she criticized Susan's childrearing, she might.

Meanings and rules about loyalty vary from couple to couple. For some, loyalty means as much togetherness as possible. For others, it means protecting one another's privacy. And for still others, it means agreeing and avoiding conflict. It's important to remember, however, that avoiding conflict can be detrimental to a relationship, as well as to the individuals in it. Resolution cannot occur when talking about whatever needs to be resolved is taboo. However a couple defines loyalty, trust in each partner's loyalty underlies a smooth-functioning relationship.

Difficulties often arise when partners view loyalty differently, and these difficulties may even lead to loss of trust. John grew up in a family that spent all of its leisure time together. When he married Lilly, he expected that she, too, would wish to spend all her free time with him. However, Lilly sometimes wanted to spend time alone, with women friends, go out when John felt like staying in, and stay in when he felt like going out. John felt rejected by these differences and began to question her loyalty and commitment to their relationship.

> Lilly: I wish you would just go on to a movie or a bookstore when I feel like staying home so I don't have to feel that I'm ruining your evening.

> John: No. I'd rather be with you, so I'll stay in when you want to.

Pam relocated away from family, friends, and a job she loved in order for Bob to pursue a career opportunity. Yet, shortly after the move he began traveling frequently, both for business and to supervise the care of his aging father. Pam, like John, believed that loyalty involves togetherness. So she was hurt when Bob did not invite her to join him on these trips. Bob, on the other hand, thought she would be bored. When she told him she wanted to go with him, he suggested she stay home and spend the time looking for a job and making friends instead.

> Bob: You'd be bored on these trips, and you know what a pain my father can be. It'd be much more interesting for you to get a job and make some friends here.

> Pam: But I married you to be with you.

Pam felt rejected and angry. She eventually began to wonder whether she could trust Bob or his loyalty. Incidentally, she also felt taken for granted.

John and Pam saw their partners behaving independently, and then labeled them disloyal for spending so much time away. Bob and Lilly, on the other hand, would not have questioned the same behaviors from Pam and John. Rather, they would have welcomed their partner's autonomy.

I almost rolled my eyes when I wrote that last paragraph. Why? Because, on the surface, it seems so obvious that these people would be more compatible with their counterpart in the other couple. However, for reasons I cannot fully explain, most people seem to pair off as these four have. People tend to choose partners who complement them or who have characteristics they wish to emulate. John may, in fact, wish to be more independent. Thus, part of his attraction to Lilly may have been a wish for her to help him become more like she is. Simultaneously, John and Lilly need his push for closeness to ensure that they have enough togetherness to maintain a relationship. Were John more like Lilly, they might spend little or no time together. Similarly, if Pam were more like Bob, he might return from his trips to discover she had created a new life that didn't include him. So she resists, in order to ensure that their lives continue to mesh. In this way, the partners in each couple interact to regulate the distance between them. I will discuss distance regulation more thoroughly later in this chapter.

When one partner behaves in ways the other views as disloyal, attachment is threatened. When one partner perceives a pattern of disloyalty, the behavior also disrupts trust. Thus, disloyalty leads to a loss of trust. For Pam and John, their partners' absence became evidence that they chose to be away. It's not a tremendous leap to suspect they preferred someone else's company, or even solitude, to Pam and John's.

Suspicion of an affair often leads to untrustworthy behavior. Snooping through drawers, wallets, e-mails, and credit card bills for evidence, when discovered by an innocent partner, leads to loss of trust in the snooper, as happened with Gary and Lisa. While a guilty partner may also claim the snooping violates trust, my point is that once trust is questioned or violated by one partner, there is a breakdown of trust in the relationship, no matter what has or hasn't actually happened.

Conflicting demands from important people may also lead to *the* fight about loyalty. Conflicting loyalties may involve one partner's parents, children from previous relationship(s), and these children's other biological parent(s). These conflicting loyalties can also be to work, friends, and activities. The situation becomes more complex when both partners have competing loyalties outside the relationship.

Each family exerts its own, unique amount of pressure on its grown children. Carlfred Broderick conceptualized this pressure as a fence around the family (5). In many families, the fence has a gate through which adult children are free to walk. Other families, however, have no gate. In these families, there is either a rubber fence, which gives the appearance of letting go but snaps the adult child back when s/he strays too far, like a rubber band, or a fence with no way out. In families without gates, romantic attachments may be seen as threats to the family and therefore a sign of disloyalty. Guilt-inducement, anger, and other negative communications are then showered upon the adult child who violates rules about family loyalty.

Eileen: I just don't know what to do about my son Paul. We've had the whole family for Sunday lunch every week since he can remember, and now that wife of his says Sunday's the only day they don't have work or do chores, and they need to have the whole day unscheduled so they can have time together. Really! Family Sundays aren't work and they aren't chores. They're relaxing and fun and being together. And they're what we do. But she has him believing he's not part of this family anymore. What do you tell someone like that?

Draw a large circle. Then add symbols for all the members of the family in which you grew up (the first letter of each person's name or their role in relation to you). These symbols can be inside or outside the circle. Have your siblings, if you have any, married and had children? If they're not already in your picture, add the families the adult children have created. Had you put them in already? Did you put them inside or outside the circle? The answers to these questions may tell you something about the fence around your family and whether you are subject to conflicting loyalties to your partner and your parents.

> Eileen: Well, Jim was in the hospital this week, they thought it was his heart again, but everything's ok. And, you won't believe what happened. We were all there: Paul, Lynn, me. And then Susie walks in with her husband. And I said, "What's *he* doing here?" And Susie looked at me and said, "Mom, he's my husband. He's here to support me." Good gracious! What were the rest of us there for?

I always see a red flag when the majority of adult children in a family have not become involved in an enduring relationship. I suspect that a message, however subtle, is prohibiting such relationships as disloyal and/or punishing those who have dared to violate the rules of family loyalty and become involved in a permanent relationship anyway.

Partners may arrive at their relationship from families who view loyalty in very different ways. Conflicts about the meaning of time together and how to celebrate events, discussed previously, are also results of such differences.

The families we grew up in also have different ways of dealing with people who marry into them. And these differences may be rather startling to the partners. Imagine what Paul and Susie's partners think of Eileen's attitudes, especially if their own families' fences had gates with signs over them welcoming the partners of adult children. Controlling and invalidating are words that come to mind, as does the notion that Eileen is trying to keep her children just that. But Eileen truly believed that her concept of family loyalty was appropriate and had in fact lived by her own rules when her parents were alive. Far from a hypocrite, she was genuinely bewildered by her children's views about family.

It's easy to feel divided loyalties in situations where the family of origin (the one we grew up in) is not letting go easily and/or is excluding a partner. Eileen inadvertently set up a situation in which her children-in-law would become competitive with her for their partners' attention. Paul's partner, for example, viewed his occasional visits to his parents to help them around their house as disloyal to her, not because of the time he spent helping his parents but because they didn't welcome her presence when he visited them. However, had he not spent this time with his parents, they would have viewed him as disloyal to them. No matter what decision he made, Paul was stuck between conflicting demands about loyalty.

Similarly, Susie's partner might have felt confused, hurt and excluded had she asked him not to accompany her to the hospital. So, Susie, too, had to choose between conflicting rules of loyalty in her relationship with her parents and her partner. She had an easy choice: she wanted him with her and so she brought him along. In many relationships, however, the partner is expected to understand, whereas no such demand is placed on members of the family of origin.

Many people view loyalty as willingness to defend a partner against attacks, as mentioned earlier in this section. Had Eileen criticized Paul's partner and he failed to defend her, she might feel he was being disloyal to her.

Annie: Your mom always criticizes my housekeeping and what I feed the kids. She's even accused me of poisoning you against her. You say she's just joking, or that's just her way, but that woman doesn't joke and "her way" hurts. I don't understand why you won't stand up for me and tell her to knock it off?

It is not at all unusual for partners to feel slighted or even ignored in favor of children from previous relationships. The needs of these children, and sometimes the needs of their other biological parent, may intrude on a new relationship. Children from previous relationships always require time and money, and have a claim on their parents' loyalty and affection. A stepparent often finds her/himself in the unenviable dilemma of knowing s/he would not respect her/his partner if s/he ignored children from a previous relationship and yet resenting how much s/he does for those children.

> Pat: I wouldn't have respected him if he'd been willing to relocate away from Sara [his daughter] for my job. But, I stayed here for her. And it cost me something, in income as well as advancement. And then he gives her whatever she wants when she's with us, in addition to all that child support we pay Louise [Sara's mother]. I'm not so sure it's a good idea for Sara to think she can have anything she wants, or that her father is buying her things out of guilt for not being there all the time. But if I say anything, he says I don't understand because she isn't my daughter. That hurts. And it feels like I'm working to support a child who isn't even mine and then I don't even have a say about how she's raised.

Even more insidious are the demands of the other parent of these stepchildren. How can it not feel disloyal when one's partner has chosen to go along with what a previous partner wants when it is not what the present partner wants? For example, a couple may have planned a weekend trip alone together. When a previous partner calls and asks them to take the kids that weekend, the kids' biological parent may be delighted. However, it is more likely that the stepparent will feel disappointed and frustrated by the intrusion of the children.

Pat: Louise just called up and said, "I need to change week-ends" and we dropped our plans to go to the beach. Last time she did this, we canceled plans with friends that were very important to me. And I get so mad at him. I think, "What about me? Don't you want to spend time with me? Don't I get some of you, too?" [Laughs] I feel so immature saying this.

Pat's position is neither enviable nor immature for several reasons. She has no good options. If Pat says, I'm so disappointed that your daughter is coming along, she sounds like she doesn't like the child. If she says, I wanted to be alone with you she runs the risk of hearing that her partner would rather be with his child than alone with her.

Pat's partner, like many divorced parents, also has no good options in terms of his loyalty to his two families. He wanted to spend time alone with Pat. And, he said he respected her career and the way she treated Sara. He also claimed that he wanted to honor her wishes, for example, to have a weekend trip alone together. Yet, Sara was also important to him, and he missed living with her. So, whenever Louise offered him extra time with Sara, he wanted to say yes.

The loyalty issue is exacerbated when one partner's time with his or her children appears to be loyalty to their other parent. Pat's partner's desire to spend time with Sara was indistinguishable from any loyalty he might have to Louise. Whenever he chose to be with Sara and incidentally accommodated Louise, he appeared to be prioritizing Louise's need for time without Sara over Pat's need for time alone with him. But appearances can be deceptive. Sometimes the loyalty is to the child rather than to the child's other biological parent. I believe this was true for Pat's partner. His goal seemed to be to spend as much time as possible with Sara, rather than to accommodate Louise.

On the other hand, some people remain terrified of a previous partner's anger and may act out of fear.

Lydia: Oh, his ex is a real witch. She calls up and says she's broke, she's spent all the child support and her job doesn't pay well, never mind that she rarely forces herself to go to it. And if he says no to giving her money, she goes ballistic. She starts screaming and calling him names. And they were married 15 years. She knows exactly what hurts him. So, he avoids these tantrums and just gives in. And then I get mad, because it feels like, hey, I'm the nice one. How come she gets whatever she wants? We can't even afford curtains for our living room and she just redecorated to help herself get over the divorce, which was six years ago, by the way.

Lydia's partner's loyalty does appear to be to his ex-wife, not out of love, but out of fear. For him and Lydia, resolving *the* fight about loyalty will depend on him first resolving his fear of his previous wife and then balancing loyalty between Lydia and his children.

Divided loyalties also arise with respect to work, friends, and volunteer activities.

Tina: During the week, he comes home, he barely talks to the kids and me, and then he's off again. I told him we needed to do some work around the house on weekends now that it's spring, and last Saturday he got up, read the paper, and then left for the rest of the day. And then I got stuck doing everything that needs doing around the house and driving the kids all over the place and making them do their homework and chores. And I work outside the home, too; it's not like I have all week when they're in school to get things done.

Rick: Tina, I lead the youth group at church and sing in the choir. Surely you agree our involvement in church is important? And I coach softball, right, because our daughter plays softball and we want to contribute. We value pulling our weight, right? And I'm on a couple of boards. I need to be for work. And we both value my paycheck, right? And I enjoy singing, so I'm also in a men's singing group in the community. It's the one thing I enjoy.

Tina: Oh, get real.

Rick: No, don't say it, I don't really like playing golf, but the doctor said I had to exercise, so I go every Saturday morning with the guys, and it wouldn't be friendly not to stay for a drink with them afterward. Anyway, Ricky's old enough to mow the lawn now. So this isn't even a hardship for you. I don't understand what all the fuss is about.

Tina's unhappiness is palpable. It is also abundantly clear that Tina doesn't feel she's particularly important to Rick. Rick's attitude suggests that he refuses to address the issue of Tina's feelings about his priorities. One wonders how long *the* fights about loyalty and importance have remained unresolved.

However, Rick clearly has some loyalty pressures, even if he tends to overdo his commitments. He was probably being truthful when he said that he and Tina value involvement at church and in the community, he has some pressure for community involvement at work, and he needs to exercise. On the surface, it is difficult to discern whether *the* fight has arisen because Rick has too many demands placed on him, he and Tina have not done a good job of assessing and prioritizing his commitments to fit their family, or Rick really wants to spend as little time at home as possible. Given that *the* fight appears to have a lengthy history, it's also possible Rick has increasingly overcommitted to avoid fighting with Tina.

Tina: Well, he's always done too much. But, yes, it's gotten worse in recent years.

Intimacy

Intimacy is a rather loaded word in our society. The Macmillan Dictionary for Children defines intimacy as "…close and familiar…very personal; private." I like this definition, because it is simple and concise, and the meaning of intimacy is often complicated and full of expectations. Keeping the meaning of intimacy in our relationships simple may help diminish *the* fight about it.

Intimate partners are emotionally and physically close in ways that are not available to the public. Emotional intimacy, or familiarity, ideally involves a sense of empathy and acceptance of the other person, as well as an ability to communicate about the relationship. Frequently, emotional intimacy involves private, nonverbal communications that may occur publicly but are only understood by the couple.

Physical closeness usually involves sexual intimacy, as well as nonsexual, affectionate touching. The decision about how much and what kinds of touching are acceptable public behaviors varies among couples and social groups.

Misunderstanding can blossom within these descriptions of intimacy. The addition of more complicated ideas about intimacy also increases the likelihood of misinterpretations about it. So, communicating about intimacy becomes an important way to avoid *the* fight about it.

Emotional intimacy. Emotional intimacy is important to both physical intimacy and communication in an enduring relationship, so I will begin by discussing emotional intimacy. Empathy, acceptance, and communication about the relationship are all essential to emotional intimacy.

Empathy entails understanding other people's perspectives and the concept that they can differ from one's own and still be acceptable. An empathetic person seems to know just how others feel. This is because s/he listens to what others say; it is not because s/he reads minds. Additionally, it is not because s/he agrees with what s/he is hearing. It only means s/he hears what is being said and accepts that this is how the person to whom she's listening views the situation. The power of believing that someone hears and understands, irrespective of agreement, is enormous. Listening is a wonderful gift that partners can give one another.

The importance of empathy seems to be widely overlooked in our society. Instead, many people ask for support, and their partners become totally confused about what is wanted from them.

> Sheila: I am so worried about our daughter. She looks so sad, and she says everything's ok but I don't believe her. And I need you to talk to me about it.

> Tom: We've talked about this, Sheila. And you've talked to her teachers about it. It's time to let it go.

> Sheila [to therapist]: This is always what happens. All I want is his support, and instead I get told to stop worrying.

> Tom: What? I'm trying to help you, Sheila.

Support is a word that can be defined in any number of ways. For example, Tom said he had been supportive by listening and making suggestions. He said he is becoming frustrated that his efforts to be supportive haven't satisfied Sheila.

> Tom [to therapist]: No matter what I do, it's not enough. And I've been trying and trying to guess what it is she wants and she won't tell me. And I do what I think she wants and sometimes it's right and sometimes it's wrong. And I'm getting pretty frustrated.

> Sheila: All I want is support.

> Tom [to therapist]: That's what she always says.

Returning to the dictionary, I think it's important to recognize that support has several meanings, all of which revolve around the four ideas of holding something upright, defending someone or something as valid, paying the costs of maintaining something or someone, and bearing a difficult situation. When someone speaks of emotional support, I assume they are talking about either being defended or held up. I doubt, for example, that Sheila was asking Tom to bear her even though he thought that she was being difficult.

The question remains, how does a partner hold the other upright emotionally? By listening? By taking on the tasks of daily living? By changing what makes the other unhappy? Changing to make another person happy is usually doomed to fail, although partners fight a great deal about whether fixing someone or something is what's meant by support.

On the other hand, suggestions that might help the partner can be viewed as support. Tom, for example, had concurred with Sheila talking to their daughter's teachers as a way to handle, or fix, her worry. He was now making a suggestion, "…let it go" about how to handle, or fix, Sheila's worry. The problem for Tom and Sheila lay in Sheila both wanting and finding herself unable to believe reassurance from Tom.

Listening, suggesting, and taking action are all specific behaviors, irrespective of whether a person considers them to be supportive. Asking for something specific from a partner may be the best way to circumvent some of the fighting about support. Being specific makes very clear what the partner who is asking for support is really wanting from the other. Had Sheila said, "I want reassurance" or "I want you to listen and validate my point of view," Tom would have understood how to support her.

Acceptance is a close companion of empathy. Like empathy, acceptance does not mean agreement. It simply means that one accepts one's partner for who s/he is. It does not mean uncondi-tionally loving everything about one's partner.

Most relationships begin with a period of infatuation. The intense feelings that accompany infatuation are supported by bio-chemical brain activity. Increased dopamine is released into the body, accounting for the general sense of wellbeing when one is newly "in love", as well as the desire to be with the beloved as much as possible. Elevated dopamine levels help obscure the distinc-tion between who the partner really is and how good it feels to be together. As a result, the partners' behavior toward one another conveys mutual acceptance and unconditional regard. Later, when they begin to see one another more realistically, each may discover less appealing characteristics in the other.

Fortunately, one can accept what s/he doesn't like about a partner.

> Marissa: When you lived alone, your apartment looked fine, not like the rat holes most of the guys I'd dated lived in.
>
> Bob: That's because I cleaned every time you came over.
>
> Marissa: No, it was more than that. After awhile, you didn't always know when I was going to drop by, and your apart-ment was still not as messy as you are now.
>
> Bob: I don't think you saw the dirt.

Probably, both Marissa and Bob are correct. Marissa may have been so impressed that Bob cared about his apartment at all that she overlooked how messy or dirty it really was. On the other hand, Bob may have been tidier when he was trying to impress her. He also may have cleaned more when she wasn't around all the time to beat him to it.

A partner who is less motivated to do a particular task may defer to the partner who is more concerned with completing the task. After awhile, the partners may polarize each other, both being more extreme together than either would be alone. If Bob and Marissa could view their disagreement as polarization about dirt and messes, then Marissa might back off from doing the housework, to give Bob time to take over some of the tasks. Allowing each other room to move along the continuum between the extreme positions of slob and cleaning fanatic would help them regain more moderate positions.

One can accept that her/his partner doesn't share identical views about housekeeping. If both approach it from positions of moderation and mutual acceptance, they can find their similarities and view their differences as not important enough to disrupt their relationship.

Communication about the relationship is the third component of emotional intimacy. Along with support, I've heard more concerns about communication than any other relationship issue. Like support, communication provides a wide range of possibilities for misunderstanding.

> Sheila: We never really communicate. He tells me what to do or what to feel and that's that.

> Tom: We communicate all the time. I tell you about my day, I ask you about yours, we talk about the kids. I don't understand what it is you want that I'm not doing.

Volumes have been written about couple communication. So, I am going to focus on two aspects of communication: communication about the relationship and differences in how men and women communicate. I am choosing these two aspects of communication because they so frequently become sources of *the* fight for couples.

Every human communication includes three components: verbal messages, nonverbal messages, and messages about the relationship between the people who are communicating. Verbal messages are the words used when people talk to one another. Verbal messages are usually easily understood. When someone misunderstands a verbal message, look for words with several connotations or which vaguely express the ideas being communicated.

Nonverbal messages include voice tone, body language, and facial expressions. Words said in a sarcastic tone of voice, with a facial grimace, or with clenched fists carry a very different message than the same words said with a smile, a relaxed posture, and a friendly voice tone. Distressed couples are much more likely to pay attention to nonverbal than to verbal messages from one another (6). So, when there is a discrepancy between these two aspects of a communication, such as reasonable words said in a sarcastic voice tone or loving words said with an angry face or arms crossed, partners in a distressed relationship will respond to the sarcasm, angry face, and defensive posture, rather than to the reasonable or loving words.

The final component of communication involves the message about the relationship. Relationship messages are conveyed both verbally and nonverbally, and are a part of every communication. For example, when one partner stands while the other is sitting, the relationship message being conveyed is power. More subtle examples, such as narrowed eyes or a shift in topics at predictable points in a conversation, may take on meanings to partners that the casual observer cannot imagine.

Linda: That's it. Did you see that?

Therapist: No. I'm not sure what you mean.

Linda: When he takes off his glasses and pinches the bridge of his nose, he's saying, "I don't want to listen to you." That's when I stop talking.

Linda's partner's gesture consistently stopped her in her tracks. Very subtly, and probably not consciously, he had learned to control the conversation by stopping it with a gesture. The relationship message from this gesture was, "I, not you or we, decide when this conversation ends." Linda harbored a great deal of anger, which he didn't understand, about this gesture for the simple reason that she heard a relationship message that excluded her from the decision about their rules of engagement.

Sometime in the 1960s, an undergraduate class at Harvard University was said to have conditioned the professor to leave the room by reinforcing, with looks of interest and nods of approval and enrapt note taking, any movement he made toward the door (7). Gradually, they got him all the way through it and out of the classroom. Whether or not this story is true, the point is well taken. Control over the lectures shifted from the professor to his students in an ongoing communication about the relationship between them.

Relationship messages can be excellent ways of communicating complex feelings that are difficult to articulate. For example, a woman tells her partner she wants help with the children, and then discourages him from providing such help. She may criticize everything he attempts to do, or say, "Not now" whenever he offers help. This discouragement may reflect her ambivalence about sharing her children. Or, it may derive from a history of anger in which she wishes to get back at him by reminding him that she believes he is incompetent or she is more competent. In either case, he may become frustrated by her relationship message: "I want something I won't allow you to give me."

Metacommunication is a technical term for communicating about communication. If a couple is able to talk about their communications, one can ask the other what s/he intended to convey and then explain its impact.

Mike: I'm confused. When you say, "Not now" every time I try to help you, I start thinking that maybe you really don't want any help. But that's not what you say; you say you want help. Please tell me which you want.

Jane: Of course I want you to help. Do I really say, "Not now" *every* time you try?

Mike: It sure seems like it.

Jane: I guess I need to pay attention to how I respond to your offers of help.

If a topic is off limits, or the partners do not have the skills to talk about their communication and their relationship, the frustration and anger on both sides may build. Jake, in the next example, may decide that he can never please Jan, and Jan may wonder why Jake doesn't try to help anymore.

Jake: I give up. Nothing I do is ever right according to you. So you can just do it yourself.

Jan: What a lovely attitude you've got.

The fight in a relationship can develop about relationship messages; for example, who is in control of what and how decisions are made. Because relationship messages are often subtly couched in nonverbal communications and partners may find ambivalence difficult to recognize, metacommunication provides a wonderful tool for pinpointing and resolving *the* fight. You'll read about how to use metacommunication in Chapter 6.

Deborah Tannen has studied and written about differences in how men and women communicate (13). Men tend to talk less, to focus on events and problem solving, and to view emotional intimacy as doing something together rather than talking about the relationship. Women, on the other hand, tend to use talking to think through ideas and concerns, to want to hear what their partner feels as well as thinks, and to view talking as a form of closeness. Heterosexual relationships may be encumbered by these differences. For example, a woman may interpret a man's silence as lack of caring, while a man may view a woman's desire for talking as demanding and unnecessary.

While not all men and women fit these patterns, they are more common than not. And the misunderstandings these differences can create are enormous.

Bill: I never think much about what I'm feeling at work. I've got a job to do, some of the people I work with are easier to get along with than others, and that's just how it is. I deal with it. I guess when someone really makes me mad I think about how I feel, but mostly I think about how to fix it. I'm not like you.

Mandy: And when I start talking about what's happening at work, you don't want to listen, you want to find a solution.

Bill: You talk and talk and go nowhere.

Mandy: It doesn't have to go anywhere. I just want someone who understands and cares about me to listen to me.

When such differences are interpreted as lack of caring, lack of empathy, or a refusal to communicate, they quickly become a source of *the* fight.

Bill: You want me to be someone I'm not. I don't care about what I'm feeling at work, it's not productive to even think about it, and you're just going to have to be satisfied with that. I'm not going to change into whoever it is you want me to be.

Mandy: Just what I need, you telling me I talk too much. You have no patience. You don't care what I go through. I'm really getting tired of being criticized for wanting to talk, like it's abnormal for people to use their voices.

Now, instead of talking about differences in communication styles, they're fighting about how furious they are with one another over their failed attempts to communicate.

Physical intimacy. Physical intimacy is an important part of any enduring relationship. It distinguishes lovers from friends. Physical intimacy includes both physical affection and sexual behavior.

It has been said that sex and money are two of the biggest sources of couple fights, or trash. This has not been the case in my experience. Rather, couples tend to let their physical relationship slide, in the face of tiredness, busyness, anger, or *the* fight. Thus, people's fights about physical intimacy are usually secondary to other problems in their relationship.

Physical affection is usually a direct reflection of emotional affection. As couples move further apart, for whatever reason, the frequency and even quality of physical affection between them may diminish. People often interpret a decrease in physical affection as withholding on the part of their partner. They then feel angry and hurt, and withhold themselves. A vicious cycle results, with greater hurt and anger escalating to greater withdrawal from physical affection.

Sexual intimacy becomes undesirable when affection wanes. The contrast between sex when the relationship was more loving and sex as an obligation or necessity leaves both partners feeling sad and alienated from one another.

Many people find it difficult to move from more to less intimacy in a relationship. So, while becoming platonic partners may be the endpoint of some intimate relationships, partners find the pain much greater than in platonic friendships that never involved sexual contact.

Many years ago, the husband in a couple I was seeing explained his feelings about sex. He said he'd prefer emotional and physical warmth as a prelude to sex, but he'd rather have sex without the warmth than no sex at all. His wife and I, being women, found this information very helpful. I think we'd both been deluding ourselves that men didn't care about the context in which sex takes place, whereas the truth is that many men, like many women, prefer sex within a loving relationship. If there is a gender difference, it is that women usually prefer no sex to perfunctory sex, whereas men are more likely to prefer perfunctory sex to no sex. In other words, neither is happy with sex in the absence of emotional intimacy, even though men are more likely than women to want to have sex anyway.

Think about the potential for misunderstanding in heterosexual couples when the man will settle for less loving sex and the woman will not. The set-up is ideal for her to conclude that men only want sex and for him to conclude that women don't want sex at all; whereas, in reality, both may want sex within a loving relationship and are simply reacting differently to the lack of it.

There are many other, less stereotypical ways in which couples violate one another's expectations about sex and, instead of communicating and seeking resolution to their distress, build walls against one another. For example,

Carrie: He never initiates. I think he's lost interest in me.

Mark: Well, you used to initiate. I thought when you stopped it meant you weren't interested anymore.

Or,

Jim: Her mind is somewhere else. I miss the closeness we once had.

Meg: I'm always so busy and so tired. It has nothing to do with how I feel about you.

Shared Values

Most people enter an enduring relationship with a list of "shoulds" for themselves and their partner and the expectation that their partner also values the items on this list. Each expects the other to share his or her goals, values, and views about the meaning of their relationship. They anticipate that they will agree on definitions of being a good partner and parent, right and wrong, and about how to use time and resources, including time together and apart and earning and spending money.

When partners disagree about the meaning of their relationship and/or do not share values, a tremendous amount of pain arises. Sometimes, lack of agreement may feel like an insurmountable barrier between the partners. At other times, partners view lack of agreement as an absence of caring or loyalty, or as a violation of trust.

It's important to recognize the futility of expecting two people to agree on everything. The family each partner grew up in heavily influences meanings, "shoulds", and values, and these families are likely to differ in many ways. In Chapter 1, I talked about rules for managing trash. Most meanings, "shoulds", and values are embedded in family rules. For example, when there is a family rule that men take out the trash, it reflects a deeper family value about traditional gender roles. Conversely, in a family that values flexible gender roles, rules about who does which chores would follow other patterns.

Most families adhere to the "golden rule"; each member is discouraged from doing to anyone else what s/he would not want done to her/himself. There also appears to be a "golden rule" of relationships, wherein each partner tends to do for the other what s/he would like the other to do for her/himself. The problem is that this is not always what the other would like done. We saw this phenomenon in the way that Lucy and Phil treat one another when one of them is sick. In another example, Pam always informs Jeff about her schedule, even when she must disrupt a busy day to do so. Since Jeff grew up in a family where members didn't keep track of one another's whereabouts, he isn't forthcoming with similar information about himself. Pam interprets Jeff's failure to reciprocate as an indication that he lacks consideration for others, and consideration is a value she thought they shared. Jeff, on the other hand, may view the information Pam provides him as unnecessary and a violation of their shared value to respect each other's work time by avoiding unnecessary interruptions.

Definitions about right and wrong can be highly subjective. Is it right or wrong to drive five miles faster than the speed limit? Obviously, it's against the law, but in many places people are not ticketed for such violations. Is it right or wrong to pay children for chores or grades? I'd say it depends on whether the payment is bribery and coercion or a reinforcement used to teach the internalized behavior associated with responsibility. Someone else might say it is either horribly bad or what good parents do.

When my older son was in middle school, he told me that he had friends whose parents were as distressed about an A- as I was about a C+. Who's right? I'm convinced expecting perfection is unrealistic and overly stressful for children and adults, and it happened that his drop in grades reflected a learning disability for which he'd previously been able to compensate. I'm also convinced that teaching a child to do her or his personal best is a valuable lesson. Where is the line between too much stress and doing one's personal best? I think it's probably situation specific, but two parents who love each other and their children and who are thoughtful about their parenting could legitimately disagree. The same may be said for other aspects of being a good partner.

There are also many myths about relationships that easily become prescriptions, or "shoulds". For example, "Relationships *should* be easier than this," "We *should* communicate more," "We *should* both want to make love on the same evenings," "We *should* agree about the importance of managing time and resources." Great goals, but are they realistic?

Notice how many times the word "should" appeared in the previous paragraph. To understand couples, I think it is important to distinguish "shoulds" from "wants". I think of "shoulds" as ideas or rules we've swallowed whole, without chewing on them and deciding whether they really are important to us. So, I know I should keep my house clean. But, what does that mean? Do I prioritize dusting, sweeping, scrubbing sinks and toilets, and organizing the clutter every day? If your answer is yes, is this housework more important than helping my children with their homework? Exercising to keep myself fit and healthy? Returning a call from a client who is in distress? Curling up with a good book at the end of a difficult day? Holding hands with my partner while we talk about our days or watch a movie?

If you take a moment to ask yourself what you want every time you find yourself thinking or saying the word "should", I suspect you would find that you would still be what you consider a good person. You probably don't want to live in squalor. But, you might find that taking care of yourself, your partner, and your children is at least as important as home care. If you give up the word "should" and shift to the word "want", you may find yourself experimenting with something in between what you "should" be doing and what you clearly want to avoid. For example, you might clean on days when you have time but prioritize exercise on days you have to choose between cleaning and exercising. That way, the house will stay reasonably clean—it won't fall apart because you're not cleaning it everyday and you'll be able to stay in shape—and you won't fall apart while caring for your house rather than yourself.

When partners discover differences in their values and meanings, they often attempt to convince the other that their own viewpoint is the correct one. The effort to convince then becomes *the* fight about shared values. And, unfortunately, it is a battle that cannot be won. Values are beyond argument.

Cliff: I think a wife should be able to listen to her husband's concerns without getting defensive.

Meagan: Concerns? Criticisms, more like.

Cliff: Will you let me finish! [Note there is no question mark, even though my word processing program is in an uproar over my punctuation. This is a great example of a relationship message: you do not have my permission to speak now.] It's important to me that when we have guests for dinner it looks like we didn't just throw things together.

Meagan: When do I ever "just throw things together"?

Cliff: Please don't keep interrupting me. [Her interruptions are relationship messages, also: you're so wrong and/or powerful that I have to challenge everything you say.] You don't even think about presentation. You just throw some lasagna, salad, and bread…

Meagan: All obviously homemade.

Cliff:…on a plate, like we live in a diner. You don't think about mixing textures or colors or making an unusual vegetable.

Meagan: Cliff, it's food I knew all the kids would eat. And, in case you didn't know, lasagna, salad, and bread are the colors of the Italian flag and are at least an American idea of what an Italian meal looks like. I really don't understand what you're complaining about.

Cliff: It's not special. It looks like what we might eat any night, just our family alone together. Food should be special for guests, and you just don't show respect for them or me when you fix a meal like that.

What Meagan hears as criticism, and what gets obscured in *the* fight about shared values, is their differing philosophies about entertaining. Meagan doesn't view unique food as more important than her guests' tastes. Cliff, on the other hand, prioritizes presentation and uniqueness as expressions of caring. How much of each partner's position is a "should" and how much is a want would require delving further into their values. *The* fight, however, is very clearly about one convincing the other that s/he is right.

Meagan and Cliff both appear to care about their guests. In this way, their values may be more similar than they think. Pointing out the similarity is also a great clinical tool for redirecting the conversation to a place where there is more good will between them. Without intervention, *the* fight would continue, and they would become entrenched and therefore polarized in their right/wrong positions about how to express caring for their guests, losing respect for each other's values in the process. In other words, as *the* fight persists, couples may appear to have fewer shared values than they really do.

On the other hand, if Meagan and Cliff were working from their shared value of caring about their guests, *the* fight might resolve.

Therapist: I'm getting the impression you both care a lot about how you treat your guests.

Cliff: Yes, that's what I'm trying to tell Meagan, that I care. And I want her to care, too.

Meagan: I *do* care, that's what she's trying to tell you.

Cliff: Yeah, but you don't think about whether it looks special.

Meagan: Listen to me. I think it's something the kids and adults will all eat and that our guests care about that. I know I do.

Cliff [warily]: Ok.

Meagan: But then all I hear from you is that I don't care enough, that I'm doing it wrong.

Cliff: I'm just trying to help you do it better.

Therapist: I think you show your caring in different ways. Cliff, you focus on whether it looks special, and Meagan, you focus on finding a solution that will make everyone happy and if it also looks good, then great. I imagine this is true about other parts of your life together as well, not just about how you treat guests; and what you're calling help, Cliff, you're hearing as criticism, Meagan.

When values are more discrepant, partners can negotiate ways of behaving that are comfortable for each, without changing the other's mind. I will discuss the specifics of how to do this in Part 3. For now, if you can learn to substitute your own "shoulds" with wants, you will be on the way.

Boundaries and Distance Regulation

Boundaries can be thought of as fences around people and relationships. As such, they help define relationships and differentiate private from public physical and emotional spaces. The ease with which boundaries can be crossed varies from extremely permeable, or easy to cross, to very impermeable, or difficult to cross.

When boundaries between people, for example, partners, are extremely permeable, the couple or family is called enmeshed. Individuals in enmeshed couples and families may experience difficulty identifying themselves separately from the other partner or other members of the family. They may subsequently lose a sense of themselves, invade each others' personal and emotional space, reveal an inappropriate amount of information about themselves to people outside the couple or family, and stand too close to others.

Alternatively, when boundaries are extremely impermeable, the couple or family is labeled disengaged. Individuals in disengaged couples and families are more difficult to get to know, may seem more private, don't know much less reveal much about their partners or others in their family, and you'd never even consider dropping by without an invitation. Like those in enmeshed situations, they lack a sense of themselves because there is so little opportunity to develop one in relation to intimate others, which is an important component of how we see ourselves.

Observers of couples and families have concluded that they and the individuals in them function best when the permeability of boundaries lies between enmeshed and disengaged. These couples and families with clear boundaries allow partners and family members more flexibility. They are capable of being close at appropriate times and separate at other times. This flexibility allows couples and families to adapt to changes, such as the birth of a child or the departure of a young adult, and to stress, such as moving or illness (8).

Developmental psychology has long held that moving away from close relationships with parents is essential to establishing oneself as an individual. Similarly, there are schools of family therapy that also hold the need for individuals to differentiate themselves from the family of origin(9). In other words, it is thought essential for us to have boundaries the rest of our family members cannot get across, at least for awhile, in order to know who we truly are. There is some evidence that this theory describes male development better than female development. Studies of girls and young women have shown that earning parental respect, rather than distinguishing oneself from parents, is sufficient to the development of a separate sense of self (10). I suspect this may be true for many men, as well, because cross-cultural studies of adolescence provide some indication that our expectation that a teenager must reject his parents may be a self-fulfilling prophecy, in other words may be contributing to distance between parents and teenagers.

In any case, prior to entering an enduring relationship a person must know who s/he is and where the boundary between her/himself and the rest of the world lies. Otherwise, partners tend to turn to one another for a definition of self.

Therapist: Tell me about what it is you value in each other.

Vicky: He has all the characteristics I don't have. He confronts the world for me.

Therapist: And Rob?

Rob: She's my gentle side.

The results can be fraught. Vicky had allowed Rob to "confront the world" for her, and so she had stopped standing up for herself, even in her relationship with him. And in allowing her to be his "gentle side," Rob had forgotten how to be gentle. So, he became verbally abusive, and she put up with being abused.

Vicky and Rob's dynamic left them vulnerable to escalating abuse. Vicky eventually developed physical symptoms of stress, which appeared linked to her fear of Rob's anger. Rob, for his part, cared about Vicky and didn't like himself when he treated her badly. Their pattern was threatening Vicky's health, Rob's self-esteem, and the relationship.

How much time a couple spends together and whether they spend it alone or with others is another indicator of their boundaries. Remember when you were newly in love and wanted to be alone with one another all the time? Did you ignore friends and family? Did they say things like, "We never see you anymore"? At the beginning of a relationship, couple boundaries are often very difficult to cross. As the relationship progresses and as the couple returns to interacting more with those outside their relationship, the boundaries may become more fluid.

This discussion brings up a question every couple must address: how close or distant will we, as a couple, be from the rest of the world? What will our relationships be to our families of origin, our friends, and the community?

Sometimes, *the* fight about couple boundaries overlaps with loyalty.

> Lisa: He wants to spend every vacation visiting his family. The kids are almost grown, and we've never had a family vacation alone, just us. I'd like some time alone as a family. But, I think his mother would have a fit, and I don't think he wants to face her.

Other times, *the* fight about couple boundaries overlaps with a sense of being respected by and important to one's partner.

> Pete: Every night she's on the phone with her friends. And then, whenever we get a sitter, she wants to go out with another couple. I don't think she likes me enough anymore to want to be alone with me.

In these examples, *the* fight is not about where the family spends its vacation or whether the couple goes out alone. It's about the boundary around the couple and how much closeness or distance the partners want between one another and between themselves as a couple and the outside world.

The concept of boundaries helps describe how a couple regulates closeness and distance within their relationship and between themselves as a couple and the rest of the world. And distance regulation is another, related source of *the* fight in a relationship.

Distance regulation involves the interactions partners use to maintain a comfortable balance of relationship closeness and distance. It includes time spent together, physical and emotional closeness, how much interaction the couple maintains with friends and family, and where and when contact occurs.

A common manifestation of *the* fight about distance regulation, or boundaries, within the couple involves one partner pursuing while the other moves away. An observer might think the pursuer wants more closeness than the distancer. But, many couples covertly assign one of these roles to each partner, and each requires that the other maintain her or his role. If the distancer stopped distancing, the pursuer would stop pursuing, and vice versa.

Sophie and Max were fairly stereotypical of this pattern. Sophie prepared lovely dinners, and Max was chronically late getting home. Sophie suggested they go to museums and shows together, while Max said museums and shows bored him. When Max initiated sex, however, Sophie wasn't interested. One explanation of Sophie's disinterest would be her anger at Max's rejection.

> Sophie: We never do anything together. You don't talk to me. You don't say, "Oh, great idea, Honey" or thank me for dinner. Mostly you don't even get home before it gets wrecked. How can you expect me to feel close enough to you to want to have sex?

A second explanation, however, is that Sophie and Max have ways of maintaining a distance in the relationship that is comfortable. Max ensures they don't become too close emotionally, and

Sophie's job is to keep a physical distance between them. They probably don't need both methods, so *the* fight is about whose method of distance regulation will prevail.

Attention to methods of maintaining distance can obscure the couple's need for some way to regulate it. Arguments about whether Max wants to do things with her or Sophie's lost interest in sex don't reverse their unsuccessful attempts to regulate distance and therefore don't resolve *the* fight about it. Acknowledging a mutual need for distance, or stronger personal boundaries, and deciding together what methods of maintaining this distance to use would help Max and Sophie stop *the* fight and accumulation of garbage around the issues of time together and sex in their relationship.

Relationship Contract

Early in a relationship, prospective partners generate agreements about what they will do and expect from themselves and each other and for the relationship as an entity. These expectations may be similar to their shared values about themselves and the relationship. However, a relationship contract differs from a list of shared values. The expectations and the values reflected in a relationship contract are those with which both partners have agreed to live.

Years ago, Clifford Sager wrote a wonderful book about marital contracts (11). He described the distinction between the overt contract a couple consciously enters into and the covert contract, which they never discuss and may not be fully aware.

An overt relationship contract can be easily described. It includes agreements about where a couple will live, who will do what, how many children they will have, and the life goals for each individual as well as for the couple. People sometimes assume telling someone about themselves constitutes a contract. However, saying,

"I want…" differs from agreeing about how to make that happen together. Only the latter is an overt relationship contract.

Assumptions partners make about what the other will do comprise their covert relationship contract. One of the most common elements of these contracts is the "fix me" agreement. Gus Napier wrote that virtually all couples agree on some level to be one another's therapists. Since even therapists cannot provide therapy for their partners, this particular agreement is doomed. But, it takes some time for couples to give up on one another as therapists. Napier linked the demise of this agreement to the infamous 7th anniversary (12).

And while the "fix-me" agreement is thriving there is plenty of room to develop *the* fight about the other's alleged contractual responsibility to fix one.

> Patsy: He never stops working. We have no life because there's never any time for one.
>
> Therapist: Tell me what it is you're missing when you say you have no life.
>
> Patsy: More of a social life. You see, I've always been shy. And Bruce is very gregarious. So, I kind of hoped he'd bring me out of my shell and I'd learn to be more comfortable in social situations. Instead, he seemed to stop caring about a social life once we were married and just threw himself into work.
>
> Bruce: Honey, I thought that's what you wanted. You didn't seem to like going to parties and having people around a lot.
>
> Patsy: No, I was really disappointed.

Covert relationship contracts leave a lot of room for misunderstanding. From Patsy's perspective, they had implicitly agreed that Bruce would "fix" her shyness. But, Bruce didn't know about this clause in their agreement. At some point, he may have been unconsciously aware of their covert agreement, but he either lost interest in or energy for changing Patsy's shyness. Or, perhaps he thought he needed Patsy's less aggressive social life to settle him down. Possibly, he thought their contract was that Patsy would "fix" his tendency to party.

> Therapist: What about you, Bruce? How was it for you to give up some of your social life after you married Patsy?
>
> Bruce: Well, that's kind of what I expected to do. To tell you the truth, I was kind of wild, maybe a little irresponsible even, before I met Patsy. So, I guess I assumed she'd change me for the better.
>
> Patsy: You're kidding. You never told me that.
>
> Therapist: You two probably never talked about these expectations.

The fight for Bruce and Patsy was about the covert contract to provide her with a social life and to simultaneously lessen his wildness. However, the true issue was obscured, and *the* fight was buried in arguments about how Bruce worked all the time.

Another potential source of conflict about the relationship contract occurs when one or both partners wish to change it. In the 1980s, a lot of couples in their 40s entered therapy fighting about what the woman would do as the children began leaving home. The women in these couples usually wanted to finish college or go to graduate school, or to begin a career they'd deferred to raise families. The men, on the other hand, often resisted these changes. While their partners expressed discontent and asserted their refusal to continue to give up what they had been willing to forego to raise children, the men were content with how things had been and reluctant to change their relationship contracts.

Jim: Who's going to take care of the house and cook dinner when you're off chasing this dream of yours?

Linda: You could do some of it.

Jim: And when am I going to have time to do your work? Remember, one of us has to earn a living. You want a change; you find a way to make it happen.

Linda: What? Hey, I never agreed to be your servant forever. It was one thing for me to clean and cook when the kids were younger and I was home anyway. But, in a year, they'll all be out of the house. What am I supposed to do then?

Jim: Garden. Go out to lunch. This is a time for you to enjoy. You don't have to work. I make enough money.

Linda: It's not about money. It's about me wanting more for my life.

Jim: Our marriage and family was always enough for you before.

Linda: Family, Jim, family. Our family is shrinking, that's the point.

Linda wanted to change the covert relationship contract. Her role was changing as their nest emptied and she experienced a concomitant loss of meaning as her children left home. But Jim was very content with how things had been. He had neither the need nor the desire to see their contract change. Hence *the* fight about whether to change the relationship contract arose.

The fight about the relationship contract usually involves either the covert contract or a change in the contract that one partner wants and the other does not. Partners sometimes overlook or suppress disagreements over the relationship contract until no choice remains but to resolve them. To stop *the* fight, partners must examine and renegotiate their relationship contract.

Power

People derive power in a number of ways. Age and experience traditionally serve as sources of power for men. For women, youth is a source of sexual power, whereas age makes us either invisible or fonts of wisdom (crones), depending upon the culture in which we live.

Size is often a source of power, with its inherent threat of taking power if it is not voluntarily given. People often express power by positioning themselves to look larger. Standing while the other is sitting, sitting on a taller chair, and wearing high heels or lifts in one's shoes are all ways of expressing power.

Class is a third source of power in our culture. Money is often the measure of status, but anything highly valued brings status. Of course, value is somewhat in the eye of the beholder. For example, a literature professor who writes a Pulitzer Prize winning book may derive a lot of status from peers and readers, even though her university salary probably falls well below that of a business executive.

Sociological studies of traditional middle-class couples have indicated that a man holds more decision-making power when he is the only wage earner. When a woman without an income makes decisions, these researchers have concluded, the man chose to delegate this decision-making to her. As an example, the couple says they both make decisions; she plans birthday parties and he purchases cars. The status of these decisions differs, however; the car holds more financial importance while the birthday party is more emotionally important. When the man was either the sole or major wage earner, the woman only planned the party because he decided he didn't want to.

Presumably, when all goes smoothly in a traditional relationship power hierarchy, both partners accept the woman's lack of power to choose which decisions she makes. Should she also feel devalued, not heard, or suffer depressive symptoms rooted in low self-esteem, the relationship waters become murkier. She may need increased power over her own life, in order to feel valued or to diminish her depressive symptoms. As she requests or insists that they renegotiate decision-making power, the man may feel a loss of power about which he is ambivalent. If there is no language for discussing the distribution of this power, *the* fight may pop up over all sorts of trash. And, with no language to discuss power in a relationship, *the* fight will not be resolved.

Many couples no longer subscribe to the traditional relationship model. But, even in two-career couples, the woman tends to marry "up" the power scale. The man may not work harder, but he is more likely than not to have a more prestigious title and/or a higher salary.

The fight about power may also arise over whose job it is to please whom, who concedes in a disagreement with no easy resolution, and who does something neither particularly wants to do. Betsy and Jim exemplify *the* fight over whose job it is to please the other.

> Betsy: When we were first together, he seemed to want to do nice things for me. He'd bring me flowers, suggest we go out to dinner on Fridays after a long workweek, and ask me how my day went—things like that. Now, he doesn't do any of those things, and I miss them.

> Jim: We've been together 20 years. Did you think the romance would go on forever?

> Betsy: Well, then, I guess you won't mind if I stop getting off the phone to ask you about your day when you come home, or stop making a dinner you like when you come back from a trip.

Jim: Yeah, I expect you to talk to me when I come home. You've had the whole day to talk to your friends. And what's wrong with making my favorite dinner when I've been away? Don't you want to welcome me home?

Betsy: What would make me "want to" do anything nice for you? I always *have* to; you don't give me any choice.

This dialogue is reminiscent of *the* fights about caring and relationship contracts. But power also sneaks in, as each views pleasing Jim to be part of Betsy's duty. There is no indication of a reciprocal expectation that Jim please Betsy. Apparently, they both assume that pleasing him is part of her job, irrespective of how she feels about him at the moment, and that she does not have the power to ask to be pleased.

If Jim were to please Betsy, this couple would view his action as a sign of caring. Jim has the power to ignore Betsy's needs without falling down on his job as pleaser. She, however, is not successful if Jim is displeased. Betsy doesn't possess the power Jim does to withhold caring if she's tired or angry or otherwise not in the mood. She also doesn't get credit for showing him how much she cares, as pleasing him is in her job description and not something extra she gives freely.

This imbalance worked well until Betsy stopped feeling cared about by Jim. Now, pleasing Jim unilaterally no longer works for her.

Another aspect of power in relationships is who concedes to whom. There are only four ways for an argument to end: the argument is resolved; the couple agrees to table the argument because it's going nowhere; or someone leaves or concedes. The concept of *the* fight suggests that arguments about a particular issue are not being resolved. Since remembering to separate from the conflict long enough to suggest a break requires a lot of practice, *the* fight is rarely tabled. So, in most relationships in which garbage from unresolved fights is accumulating, someone is eventually leaving or conceding.

> Susan: He always leaves. We get going in an argument, and he just walks out.

> John: Well, it's going nowhere. What's the point of staying?

Or, alternatively,

> John: When she gets angry, what she's saying gets more and more irrational and there's no point in arguing, so I just say, "OK" and then at least the arguing stops and we can move on.

When one partner feels s/he has no power, physical symptoms emerge for physiological or emotional reasons. These symptoms often bring a measure of power.

Bill worked 60 hours a week or more and was also involved in volunteer activities within the community. Patty begged him to spend more time at home, helping her with the children's evening routine, playing with them so she could have some time to herself, and spending time with her. She also worried about the impact of Bill never being at home on their children's mental health. Bill made promises about spending more time with the family, but invariably broke them. In other words, he maintained the position of power in deciding how much time he, as well as Patty, would devote to the family.

When Patty was 41 years old, she had her first migraine. Her physician was uncertain as to whether her migraines were a result of hormonal changes or stress. Their functional value quickly became clear: after Patty started having migraines, Bill was home more, the children were quieter, and the demands on Patty diminished. The migraines also took away her energy for being angry with Bill. The migraines returned some of the power to Patty; she was now able to force Bill to be more involved with the children.

The process of deciding who does something neither wants to do reveals a lot about the couple's dynamics and values. Some couples agree to divide these tasks. Others, however, get mired in struggles about whether the tasks need to be done at all and if so, who must do them.

Bob and Barb lived in the same town as his family. Barb worked 36 hours a week as a nurse, while Bob was a senior partner in a large accounting firm. Barb and Bob were committed to spending time with their two school-aged children in the evenings.

> Bob: I've told her not to worry about how the house looks if someone from my family drops by during the week. We just can't be worrying about that. We have way too much else to think about and, anyway, it's not important to us. But, when someone from my family calls to say they're coming over, Barb flips out. I've reassured her they don't care how the house looks; they want to see the kids and us. I don't want to get caught up in her frantic cleaning, and I don't know what else to do.

> Barb: Well, I can't very well say, don't bother us during the week. But, it's so embarrassing when there are newspapers and clothes all over the floor and we haven't even washed the dinner dishes at 8:00. So, what can I do? I run around like a maniac cleaning up, and then I'm mad because I haven't spent the time with my kids and mad at Bob when he's with them instead of helping me. And, of course, they won't think badly of him if they see he lives in a mess. They'll feel sorry for him that he's stuck with a wife who can't keep it together.

> Bob: No they won't. They know how hard you work and what a good mother you are.

Barb: Yeah, but your mother never worked outside the home. And your sisters' houses never look like ours. They're bound to compare me.

Bob: You weren't there when my mother had kids at home. It wasn't so great. It looked like a house full of kids. And neither of my sisters has kids.

Barb: Bob, you just don't understand. If you want to help me, help me pick up the place or do the dishes.

Although Barb believed strongly in her choice to prioritize time with her children over housekeeping during the week, concern about her in-laws' judgment threw her into turmoil. And the ensuing argument with Bob grew into *the* fight about Bob having the power not to do what Barb considered essential. However, it also could be argued that if Bob gave in to Barb's demands, he would cede power to Barb to decide whether he must do something he considered dispensable.

Whether to concede poses an interesting dilemma for couples. *The* fight about power arises when one or both believes s/he must concede on important issues. However, conceding on issues that are not important is a reasonable way to avoid or resolve conflict. If it seemed inconsequential to Bob to pick up the newspapers and clothes or wash the dishes immediately after dinner, then what would he lose if he did it to help Barb feel better about visits from her in-laws? When a partner is reluctant to concede unimportant issues, it may be a red flag for *the* fight about power.

Over-functioning can also be a source of power. On the one hand, it gives the appearance that one partner is extremely competent while the other is dependent, perhaps incompetent. Even as the under-functioning partner may be relieved of some responsibilities, s/he is simultaneously deprived of power to make decisions regarding the couple's life together. S/he may also be receiving messages of devaluation, which trigger anger and subsequently lead to *the* fight about power.

Kristin: He never helps around the house. I can't even get him to load the dishwasher.

Kurt: Why should I bother? You always come along behind me and rearrange the dishes, so you might as well do it in the first place.

While Kristin viewed her way of loading the dishwasher as superior to Kurt's, her insistence that he load it her way wrested power from him; and he resisted.

Kurt: You know, I don't care whether I load the dishwasher. But I really would like to give my son a bath and put him to bed.

Kristin [to therapist]: I can't leave him alone with our son in the tub. He doesn't pay any attention. He'll wander off and the baby will drown.

Kurt: Come off it, Kristin. You know I'm not going to wander off and leave a two year old alone in the bathtub. You just always have to be right. And, you always have to be in charge of everything.

Kristin's remark to the therapist provides an excellent example of how the over-functioning partner obtains power over things that are important to both. Kristin and Kurt also exemplified how *the* fight about power plays out for a couple when one partner over functions.

Conclusion

In this chapter we examined nine issues about which couples fight. The examples in each section not only illustrated the issue covered in that section but also made clear that issues overlap to a great extent.

We'll now turn to the work of identifying and resolving *the* fight in your relationship. But first, I want to tell you more detailed stories about four couples, to bring the nine issues, or themes, to life. These couples are composites of couples with whom I've worked, as well as people I've known in my personal life. They further illustrate the point that *the* fight in a relationship usually includes more than one of the nine issues discussed in this chapter.

3

Stories about Couples and their Fights

In this chapter, we'll examine four couples and *the* fight in each of their relationships. These couples illustrate the nine issues that underlie *the* fight in any relationship. The trash that produces *the* fight, however, differs from couple to couple. Despite different trash, or manifestation of *the* fight, unresolved arguments about unaddressed issues have led to an accumulation of relationship garbage for all four couples.

The process by which *the* fight can transform trash of all kinds into relationship garbage will become apparent as you read about Alan and Samantha, Adele and John, Pete and Shelly, and Brad and Serena. These couples' histories illustrate the trash, *the* fight, and the garbage in their relationships.

These couples were created to exemplify the range of issues underlying *the* fight, styles of identifying *the* fight, and outcomes of identifying and resolving *the* fight. They are not intended to reflect the percentage of couples that experience any given outcome.

Alan and Samantha: Years of Fighting

Samantha and Alan are in their early to mid-40s and have been engaged in *the* fight since their older child was born 12 years ago. Samantha is soft-spoken. Alan appears more gregarious. They both appear happy, but their calm is only on the surface. When disturbed, Samantha raises her voice and Alan becomes curt and sarcastic.

Samantha and Alan met in graduate school and dated for 3 years before marrying. Both wanted to remain single so they could pursue their careers. However, neither wanted to stop seeing the other; and by the time they began looking for jobs, they had decided to stay together and make whatever career concessions were necessary for the relationship to work.

The early years of their relationship were characterized by mutual respect for the other's work and accomplishments. They shared many friends and had an active social life. Neither believed that a woman should sacrifice her career to support her husband's. So, when Samantha was offered her dream job, they agreed she would take it and Alan would follow her.

After they moved, Alan's career stagnated. He did not find a particularly challenging or prestigious job. Samantha worked long hours, and Alan retreated into hobbies and sports. They had no network of friends, as they had had in graduate school, so their social life was minimal. Samantha began to feel isolated and bored when she was at home with Alan, wondering where the man she had married had gone. Since she didn't want work to consume her whole life, she began to make her own friends at work.

Samantha and Alan continued to do a great job of delegating household tasks. They established routines for taking care of their home that not only worked, but also felt equitable. They didn't fight much, but Samantha felt they were drifting apart. Eventually, she consulted a therapist.

During a brief course of therapy, Samantha and Alan agreed that they needed to spend more time together. They talked about their personal and career goals and re-established themselves as a couple. They felt therapy had been successful, that they were once again working together toward a shared future, and agreed that they wanted to remain married. After about six months of feeling closer and enjoying one another's company more, they decided that their relationship was strong enough to sustain a child.

After their first child was born, Samantha surprised herself by not wanting to return to work. She even offered to move so that Alan could find a more fulfilling job. But Alan was hesitant to make a major change, and at his insistence, Samantha continued working 30 hours each week. Since Samantha wanted to be home with her children, she cheerfully took on a large share of child-care responsibilities. As time went on and Alan's career progressed while hers foundered on the mommy track, she found herself doing more and more of the home care, as well.

Alan and Samantha became busy with their children's needs and activities, and spent less time together. Alan's job stress increased, and he once again retreated into sports and hobbies when he had time.

Samantha found herself lonely and angry at Alan's withdrawal. He, on the other hand, felt that he wasn't doing anything new. He told her she'd known from the beginning that he needed time for himself and felt it was unfair for her to suddenly expect him to change.

Whenever Samantha suggested they get a regular sitter and go out together, Alan declined. Samantha felt rejected and hurt. For his part, Alan experienced Samantha's attempts at closeness to be demanding and critical of his need for alone time; he did not experience Samantha's gestures as either warm or loving.

Additionally, Alan felt that Samantha was not holding up her end of their bargain, now that she was no longer working full time. The house was often disorderly. When he complained to her about it, she would say she had no time, after work she was busy with the kids and could only do housework on weekends. She suggested

Alan help more. He refused, pointing out that he still worked full-time. Needless to say, the weekends were characterized by tension and fighting.

As the children grew older, Samantha and Alan agreed they could help around the house. Alan wanted a chores schedule, with consequences for failing to complete assigned tasks. Samantha's style involved noticing something needed to be done and telling one of the children to do it. The success of her approach began to diminish as the children entered preadolescent years and wanted more autonomy. Alan, who remained angry about the state of the house, felt that it was Samantha's job to develop the schedule of chores for the children and make it work. He again suggested she create a formal schedule. Samantha agreed and asked him to work on it with her.

By this time, Alan was entrenched in his position: he was holding up his end of the relationship by working full-time outside the home and it was therefore not part of his job to help (Alan's word) Samantha create a chores schedule. Samantha felt that for her to assume full responsibility for the home and children was unfair, since she still worked 30 hours a week at a professional job. She also insisted she couldn't enforce a chores schedule without Alan's participation.

The trash, or content, of their fights involved the question of who was going to take the initiative in getting the children to do their chores and, incidentally, other tasks that needed doing, such as lawnmower repair. Alan refused to participate in planning or enforcing a chores schedule, claiming that he was already con-tributing enough. Samantha, who wanted his assistance, refused to take responsibility for developing a method of ensuring the children would help around the house, claiming that Alan was undermining any attempts on her part by refusing to participate. Variations on this theme included accusations about how little the other did and about how disappointed each was in the other as a partner. Whatever they argued about led quickly to a flare-up about Samantha working part-time after the children were born.

The fight in Samantha and Alan's relationship included elements from three of the nine themes discussed in Chapter 2: power, the relationship contract, and shared values. Although they overlap, we'll examine these themes separately.

Power. Alan and Samantha reached a standoff about who would take responsibility for getting the children to help around the house *and* whether this needed to be done in a structured way. They were also at a standoff about who would decide who would assume responsibility for getting the children to help around the house. Alan said it was Samantha's job. Samantha said not only was the household not solely her responsibility, but also that she couldn't succeed in organizing the children without Alan's help.

Three aspects of the power issue emerged here. The first involved deciding whether a structured chores schedule was needed. The second concerned the question of who was responsible for planning and enforcing that schedule. And the third entailed who decided who was responsible for planning the chores schedule. This last was subtler and yet probably even more important than the other two.

In couple fights, it's often apparent what each partner wants to talk the other into doing. However, this struggle over who has the power to decide what the other will do may not be addressed directly. All one heard directly from Alan and Samantha was a struggle about whether Alan was going to participate in developing and implementing a chores schedule. However, Alan and Samantha also fought about who had the power to decide whether Alan participated. Neither addressed this other struggle.

Although Samantha continued to work outside the home, she lost a tremendous amount of power, especially relative to the number of hours she continued to work outside the home, by shifting from a full-time to a ¾-time job. She had been on a career path that required a full time commitment, and so the "mommy track" reduced her earning potential and the prestige of her career. Additionally, she changed their relationship contract, and Alan was clearly unhappy about both the change in the contract and her apparent loss of interest in her career.

Listening to Alan and Samantha's words, one might suggest that whoever wanted a chores schedule more needed to initiate it in the absence of agreement to share planning. While this recommendation makes intuitive sense, it only addresses the trash and not *the* fight. *The* fight was not about a chores schedule, but rather about who decided who would take responsibility for it. *The* fight could only be resolved if they talked about power, rather than chores.

The fight about power might sound like this:

Samantha: This is an opportunity for us to work together, like we used to, and develop a chores schedule and a way of enforcing it that works for our family.

Alan: That's a smokescreen, Samantha. You've opposed a chores schedule in the past, and now you're trying to get me to do the work for you? Forget it. It's your job, not mine.

Samantha: It won't work unless the kids know we're both committed to it.

Alan: I didn't say I wasn't committed to it. I just said it's your job to create and enforce it. If I have to, I'll back you up.

Samantha: I think it's *our* job as parents?

Alan: Well, I disagree. I do enough since you stopped working.

Samantha: What?! I wanted to stop working, but oh no, you didn't want that. Too bad for you, because if I were home like I wanted to be we could talk about my taking over responsibility for everything.

This was not a resolution, but rather a first step toward it. In this scenario, Alan and Samantha brought up two of the issues underlying *the* fight, although it's not clear they were aware they had.

<u>Relationship contract</u>. A second issue underlying *the* fight involved Samantha's profession as part of their relationship contract. When they met, both were committed to pursuing serious careers. They enjoyed talking about their work with one another, sharing ideas, and giving feedback. Each felt that s/he benefited from the other's input. Additionally, these discussions were part of the closeness they felt to one another. When they'd discussed having a family, Samantha never indicated that she might not continue to prioritize her career. Rather, they expected their income to cover care for very young children at home and talked about the benefits of daycare for preschool-aged children (independence, social skills).

When Samantha wanted to stop working after the birth of their first child, Alan saw her discarding an important component of their relationship. Hurt and anger augmented his belief that she was failing to live up to her part of their relationship bargain. He also felt burdened financially, both by her desire to stop working and then by the decreased future earning potential that accompanied her shift to a part-time career path. Alan then began to withdraw from home care and emotional intimacy, retaliating for Samantha abandoning her part of the relationship contract by reneging on his own.

Samantha said she viewed Alan as being inflexible about her desire to stop working. She said she was surprised by this inflexibility, as well as angry that he didn't seem to care how she felt. As time went on and Alan was doing less than he had before they had children, Samantha's anger escalated. The 10 hours a week she no longer worked outside the home had turned into a 60 hour a week job managing home and children.

The fight about the relationship contract might sound like this:

> Samantha: Since I stopped working full time, everything else has become my responsibility. It's unfair, and I feel burdened by your refusal to help me.

> Alan: Since you stopped working full time I feel burdened with financial responsibility and angry that you don't seem to feel you need to help me.

> Samantha: Help you? You'd think I'd stopped working altogether. I still earn 75% of what I earned before the kids were born. It's not like you're the only one earning money in this family. Plus, I now handle all the finances *and* homecare *and* responsibility for the kids.

> Alan: Don't deceive yourself. If you hadn't gone on the mommy track, you'd be making a lot more by now.

> Samantha: Is money that important to you? It never was before.

> Alan: No. I'm mad because we never talk about our work anymore. It's like it's not important to you. You've turned into someone you said you didn't want to be.

Shared values. Alan and Samantha's fight illustrated a struggle about the definition of a good partner. They agreed that a good partner shares responsibilities, even though they disagreed over how well the other was achieving this objective. Both also agreed that a good partner displays empathy. However, Alan expected a good partner to empathize with how overwhelmed he felt being the primary income earner, as well as with his need for time to manage his stress. Samantha, on the other hand, wanted Alan to empathize with her desire to stay home with their children. And she believed a good partner would have been receptive to changing the relationship contract when she asked. Finally, Alan and Samantha struggled with how much time good partners would wish to spend together.

The values underlying *the* fight in Alan and Samantha's relationship included responsibility, empathy, flexibility, and togetherness. While they both valued responsibility and empathy, they disagreed about whether flexibility and togetherness were also traits of a good partner. They did share a common belief that the other had not lived up to their criteria, individual or shared, for a good partner.

The fight about shared values might have sounded like this:

Samantha: A good husband would be devoted to teaching his children responsibility by example and so would help me plan and enforce a chores schedule. He would also not want me to feel so overwhelmed and responsible for everything.

Alan: A good wife wouldn't change her mind about her career. She also wouldn't keep demanding that I do more and more, while she is not doing what she said she would do.

Prior to identifying *the* fight in their relationship, Alan and Samantha continued to fight about the trash. With each unresolved repetition of *the* fight, more garbage accumulated.

Samantha: It seems like all you care about is being right. You don't care what the kids learn about responsibility, or how hard my life is. It's all about you being right.

Alan: And you are devious, Samantha. First you don't care about your career, now you're trying to foist responsibility for the house and kids onto me. Do you want to be completely dependent and irresponsible? If that's what you want, I don't even know you anymore.

So now Samantha and Alan were dealing with the trash about the chores schedule; *the* fight about power, the relationship contract, and values; and the garbage about whether Alan is more concerned about being right than being a good husband and father and whether Samantha is devious and dependent. This garbage derived from *the* unresolved fight about power, contract, and shared values issues. And this garbage produced yet more arguments that couldn't be settled without resolving *the* fight.

Alan: How can you say all I care about is being right? I care about our family. But I've also learned I need to care about myself, or you'll run all over me.

Samantha: Run all over you? Be devious? No wonder you don't know me anymore. All you see is some creation from your own mind. I don't think you've ever forgiven me for my reaction to being a mother, for loving the children more than my career. And you're never going to stop punishing me, are you? No matter what kind of an ogre you have to make me in your mind. And even if it hurts the kids.

Alan: Great, Samantha. Now you're saying I'm crazy and I don't care about my kids.

The fight will continue, with an increasing accumulation of garbage from escalating hurt and anger, until Alan and Samantha either resolve the three issues underlying it or give up on each other as reasonable partners. And as is now obvious, as *the* fight continues more garbage accumulates. This garbage, incidentally, provides evidence that, in fact, each had married an irresponsible person who violated contracts, was insensitive and manipulative, and grabbed for power.

And this is how a fight about whether children must clean up their rooms becomes a fight about whether two people can stay together. Couples don't break up over messy children's rooms or overflowing wastebaskets. Nor do they present for therapy to talk about the states of their children's rooms or their wastebaskets. Therapy and divorce are too painful, time-consuming, and expensive. Couples arrive at a therapist or attorney's office because they are on the verge, if not over the edge, of losing hope that their partner can be who they thought s/he was.

Adele and John: The Insurmountable Problem

Adele and John had recently turned 50. John was high-powered, driven and focused. Adele appeared sociable and competent. However, one quickly discovered she lacked confidence.

When Adele and John met, they were living in a large urban area more than 500 miles from their families of origin. John was pursuing a career that required him to live in a large city, while Adele had decided when she was quite young that she needed to get away from her family. She had just graduated from college; he was a couple of years older.

John was an only child. His parents' marriage had begun deteriorating when he was about 12. They would fight almost daily. The fights would end without being resolved, and his father would "storm out" of the house. John would be left to comfort his mother, playing games and watching television with her to distract her. His parents "finally" divorced while he was in high school. After the divorce, he continued to spend as much time as possible with his mother, listening to her anger, sadness, and anxiety about her future. He felt obligated to be there for her, even though he would have preferred to be with his friends, some of whom had divorced parents and understood what he was going through.

When John applied to colleges, his mother encouraged him to do what was best for him. He decided to go away to school, even though he was uncomfortable leaving her. Several years later, she remarried. John then felt comfortable remaining away from home to pursue his career.

Adele was the youngest of three sisters. Her mother was unhappy, but rather than making changes in her own life, blamed her problems on her husband and daughters. Adele described her mother as critical, frequently comparing Adele unfavorably with her older sisters.

The oldest sister moved into a dormitory at a nearby college when Adele was 13. Adele loved visiting her at the dorm and envied her sister. She felt her sister squandered the advantage of being out of the house by phoning home almost daily and visiting every other weekend. When her middle sister followed the same path, Adele vowed she would leave home differently. She decided she would go far enough away to avoid the frequent phone calls and visits. And so she chose a university more than 500 miles away in a large city where she could justify staying after she graduated.

After they finished college, both of Adele's older sisters married and continued to live near their parents. Each sister spoke to her mother daily and visited every weekend. Both sisters were angry with Adele for leaving. They accused her of neglecting her responsibility to help them with their parents, as though these apparently healthy 55 year olds were elderly and dependent.

After Adele left for college, her mother called her every Saturday. During these phone conversations, she complained about Adele's father. She also complained about the two older sisters, enumerating the mistakes they made raising their children and dealing with their husbands. Finally, she shared her disappointment in Adele. Claiming concern about Adele's sense of family and its impact on her ability to be a good wife and mother in the future, she would berate her for living so far away and not visiting more often. Adele said it was as though she were an only child of ailing parents, ignoring their needs for more care.

Adele's family's get-togethers were characterized by fighting and tense silences. Her mother would criticize everyone present, including her grandchildren. Or, someone would displease her mother, and she would lapse into disapproving silence. The sisters would then fight about whose fault it was, often targeting Adele for living so far away.

For Adele, these interactions were quite guilt provoking. She never felt she was doing anything well enough to please her mother and sisters. After she and John married and had children, she also felt she should protect her children from these family gatherings by declining to go. Under pressure, however, her resolve failed.

Observing her family when they were together confirmed Adele's suspicion that it was easier for her to deal with them from a distance. When away from them, she could see how her mother and sisters enjoyed dissecting her and her faults. When she talked to them on the phone or visited, however, she began to believe what they said about her.

John had been very sympathetic about Adele's family from the beginning. He always listened and took her side when she described the latest horrors. When he began accompanying her to visit her family, they treated her, though not one another, better. Adele felt safe and protected by John. John, for his part, was happy to help her manage her relationship with her family. He recognized that her mother and sisters' critical remarks were their way of interacting and didn't take it personally. He hoped he could help Adele view them the same way.

Adele also continued to be drawn into the family squabbles whenever she spoke to her mother or sisters and when she visited them. Then she felt badly about herself and questioned her decision to interact with her family. Additionally, whenever it was time to plan holidays or vacations, Adele's family pressured her to spend the time with them. Over the years, Adele and John argued about their need for family vacations and holidays apart from her parents and sisters and occasionally about John's desire to see his family.

Over the years, John became increasingly frustrated with Adele and her ongoing problems with her family. On some level, he believed she was rejecting his help and at the same time undermining his ability to help. The situation left him feeling angry, hurt, and lacking an ability to help the women he loved. After all, he told himself, the only person who had truly helped his mother was her second husband.

Meanwhile, Adele and John had had three children. After the birth of their first child, they had agreed that Adele would stay home to care for their children. Adele loved being a homemaker. She rejoiced in her children. And she was proud that she had created a home that was nurturing and loving, as opposed to the critical and demanding environment in which she'd been raised.

As their youngest child approached high school graduation and made plans for leaving home, Adele, though sad to see him go, began to think about what she'd like to do. She thought about returning to school or opening a teashop. She appreciated the flexibility John's income gave her to do either one.

John, on the other hand, viewed the departure of his children as a lessening of the financial burden for supporting the family. While he loved his work, he was growing tired of the pressure of his high-profile job. He found himself fantasizing about a slower paced life in a smaller town. Not surprisingly, he began exploring opportunities and found that a former colleague with whom he had enjoyed working had opened an office in a town 10 miles from where Adele grew up. Mike's business was doing well, and after several months of talking and thinking it over, he invited John to join him.

When John presented this opportunity to Adele, she was incredulous.

Adele: I can't believe this. Why didn't you tell me?

John:Why do you think I didn't tell you? I expected you to do exactly what you're doing. Who'd want to subject himself to this?

Adele: Oh, please. You make a huge decision that affects me without asking me, and you expect me to smile sweetly and say, 'Thank you, Dear.'

John: No. I expect you to say, "After all these years of working yourself half to death for us, I'm glad you want to slow down and enjoy life with me, your wife."

Adele: Couldn't you slow down and enjoy life here? And what about me? For the last 25 years, everything I've done has been for you and the kids. Now I'm going to have time to pursue my own dreams, and you want me to go back to [town] and deal with my parents and sisters? And, by the way, when did you think they'd leave me time for you? "…Enjoy life with me…"? That's a joke.

John: Oh, come on, Adele. First, learn to say no to your mother and sisters. And then, don't forget you could have gone to work any time you wanted to, so don't make me the heavy on that. It was a decision we made together. You loved every minute of being a stay-at-home mom.

Adele: Yes, I loved staying home with the kids, but I paid a price for it. And I also have things I want to do now that they're grown. You know that. I've at least done you the courtesy of telling you my dreams.

John: You can open a shop where we're moving. Or even go back to school.

Adele: In case you hadn't noticed, my dreams don't include following you back to a place I put a lot of energy into escaping from. What am I going to do there? Have lunch with my charming sisters? Listen to my mother list my faults every day on the phone? Or, better yet, visit them and watch my blood pressure rise from the tension? Charming, John! I can't wait.

John: This is a lovely side of you, Adele. Twenty-five years, and I had no idea you're this selfish.

Adele: *Me* selfish?

To complicate things for Adele, her parents and sisters had been pressuring her to move closer as her parents aged. With the added pressure from John's wish to downsize his career, she began to waiver. Perhaps adult children *do* owe it to their parents and siblings to live close enough to help, she told herself. Perhaps her parents had mellowed, although she doubted it; they were only 80, and neither suffered from dementia or other serious physical problems. And, she reminded herself, her mother's criticism hadn't abated with age. On the other hand, Adele's mother and sisters were always saying that her parents wouldn't be alive forever. Perhaps I *am* being selfish to insist on staying away, even though I know it will be difficult to live so close, she thought. She also wondered whether she owed it to John to move so he could simplify, irrespective of her feelings about the location.

Meanwhile, after this argument, John began to have doubts about what he was asking from Adele. He didn't want her to be drawn into her mother and sisters' squabbles. He began to examine the impact of the move on Adele's happiness and on their marriage more thoroughly.

The fight in Adele and John's marriage contained elements of four of the nine issues discussed in Chapter 3: relationship contract, respect and importance, loyalty, and boundaries. Again, let's examine each theme separately, even though they overlap.

Relationship contract. Adele and John developed an overt relationship contract. They established that Adele would stay home with their children, while John pursued the career he wanted. They also agreed to a covert clause stipulating that they would not move closer to Adele's family. And this contract worked quite well for 25 years.

The problem developed when their childrearing years drew to a close. Their dialogue suggested that they'd never talked about what their lives would be like after their children left home. While Adele shared her thoughts about her options, they had not addressed John's wishes or the impact of this new stage of their family life cycle on their relationship contract.

Therapist: Did you two ever talk about what you expected for your marriage after your children left home?

Adele: Not really. John seemed pretty happy in his work, at least he never said he wasn't.

Therapist: So, you assumed he'd want to keep doing the same job after the kids graduated from high school?

Adele: Yes. And I figured I'd need something to do. It didn't take long for me to get excited about a couple of possibilities.

Therapist: John, what about you? Do you remember whether you and Adele ever talked about what you wanted after your children moved out?

John: No, Adele's right, we didn't. We've talked about retirement some. But that's still awhile off. I didn't think we'd have any choices till the kids were out of college. But then this opportunity with Mike came about, and when I looked at the numbers I discovered that between a lower cost of living and Adele wanting to work, we could help the kids with school *and* I could get out of the rat race.

Therapist: It sounds like the two of you have agreed that, since you've been the breadwinner, John, you make your own career choices?

John: Pretty much, yeah.

Therapist: Adele?

Adele: Yes, I guess I agree. But he only ever made one choice, and I knew about it and liked it.

Therapist: Did you also agree before you married that you'd never move back to the area where Adele grew up?

Adele: I thought it was obvious to him I didn't want to live there.

John: Yes, but you've been gone over 30 years.

The covert contract apparently contained a clause that John, as the major breadwinner, got to choose his job. Adele assumed that he would neither choose to change jobs nor wish to move back to the area where she grew up. Possibly, another clause in their covert relationship contract specified that John would not change his mind either about his career or where to live. Adele's statement suggested that they had not agreed about what to do if John changed his mind, at least prior to his retirement.

This covert contract only became a problem when John wanted to move closer to where Adele had grown up. Had John wanted to return to that area before the children left home, *the* fight about their relationship contract would have arisen then. Had John chosen to change jobs and move elsewhere, *the* fight about their relationship contract might not have arisen at all.

Although the argument included an exchange about Adele having a turn to do what she wanted, Adele and John agreed about her options. Some couples do fight about whether a partner who has been at home raising children will return to work after the children leave home. But Adele's upset about having her turn at a career outside the home appeared tangential to *the* fight about whether John was violating the relationship contract by suggesting they move closer to Adele's family.

Respect and importance. Adele's sense of her decreasing importance to John became a second issue underlying *the* fight about where they live. Adele believed John had agreed to prioritize her need to remain a safe distance from her family. John honoring this agreement signified Adele's importance to him and his respect for her.

> Adele: You used to listen when I talked about them. And you'd say, "Yes, Honey, it's ridiculous how your mother can find your most sensitive, insecure spot and attack it." Why are you asking me to subject myself to more of her?
>
> John: Adele, you're 50 years old. It's time to stop letting her opinions matter so much to you.
>
> Adele: That's easy for you to say.
>
> John: You know how your mother can't say anything about anybody that isn't critical. You've got to stop thinking it's about you.
>
> Adele: It doesn't matter to you, does it?
>
> John: What?
>
> Adele: It doesn't matter to you how miserable this move will make me.

Adele said it explicitly. She believed her concerns about living near her family no longer mattered to John, or at least weren't important enough to stop him from making this move.

John: Of course I don't want you to be miserable, Adele. I just think—how many times do I have to say this?—it's time to stop listening to her.

Although John obviously cared about Adele, he had stopped placing her difficulties with her family above his career needs, leaving her with the sense that she was not as important to him as she once was.

Did John respect Adele's feelings about living near her family?

John: Yeah, you've got a right to your feelings. It's just that they're so irrational.

Adele: Irrational? You're calling me irrational?

John: I want to help you; I've always wanted to help you, but I can't seem to. And you won't, or can't, help yourself.

John had been a rescuer with both his mother and Adele. It was his job to understand Adele's conflicting upset and loyalty to her parents and somehow save her from allowing her guilt to draw her into the tangle of her family of origin. He had done so by listening, with verbal feedback, and by concurring in a geographic solution. As time passed, however, he concluded that, no matter where they lived, only Adele could rescue herself. When he began to give up the role of rescuer, likely assigned to him in their covert relationship contract, Adele experienced the change as a diminishment of her importance to him.

Tensions between Adele and her family then expanded to include tensions between Adele and John about her family. Specifically, John became more frustrated with the situation, and Adele correctly interpreted his frustration as a new unwillingness to be influenced by her feelings about her family. His desire to move left her wondering whether he respected her and whether she'd lost importance to him. If they focused on the move rather than on whether John respected Adele and whether she was, in fact, less important to him than she once was, *the* fight would not be addressed and the issues of respect and importance would generate more garbage like the pending argument about Adele's reaction to John's accusation that she is irrational.

Loyalty. The issue of loyalty also underlies *the* fight in Adele and John's relationship. Adele's family has apparently intruded on vacations and holidays, as well as on Adele's self-esteem and peace of mind. So, there remained the question of Adele's priorities: was her first loyalty to John and their children, or to the family in which she grew up?

> John: I wonder sometimes, as much as they upset her, whether their opinion of her isn't more important to her than what I think.

> Therapist: Say more about that.

> John: Well, as I've said, if they want us to spend holidays and vacations with them, Adele may complain about it but she never says no. And if I say, "Let's do something else," she says, "We can't" and sometimes even gets angry with me for suggesting it.

> Therapist: As though you've been disloyal?

> John: Possibly. Yeah, I guess so. But, sometimes it also feels like the kids and I aren't as important to her.

Here's respect and importance from John's perspective, mixed in with the issue of loyalty.

> John: If I say, "Let's go to the beach without your family" or, "Let's have a cozy Christmas at home this year," she doesn't seem to care whether it's what I want to do. It's like, if they want something, they get it. If the kids and I want something

that conflicts with what they want, it's too bad for us; her parents always come first.

Adele: But you know that's not because I want to be with them. And it's not that you're not important—good Heavens, how can you say that? It's that it's not ok to say no to them.

John: My point exactly: it's ok to say no to us. It feels like we're expendable to you, Adele.

"It's not ok to say no to them." This statement strongly suggested the presence of a family rule: never say no to us, even when you are grown and have a family of your own that requires your attention. This rule also includes a relationship message about loyalty: your first loyalty must always be to us.

Adele was in an unenviable position. What John described about loyalty was the dilemma in which Adele found herself even before she and John were together. As much as she wanted to break free from her family, the rules about loyalty extracted tremendous guilt for her attempts at independence.

The presence of a loyalty rule for grown children suggests the existence of a boundary issue, as well. For, if the family in which one grew up does not allow one to move fully into the family one creates as an adult, where does the boundary between these two families reside?

Boundaries. *The* fight about boundaries for Adele and John overlapped *the* fight about loyalty. Whatever boundary separated Adele's two families unmistakably converged in her. When the boundary was clear, it tore her apart, as one side ignored the needs of the other. When it was vague, as with respect to the proposed move, she became confused. Where was the boundary between her mother and her husband's needs, except in geographical distance?

Where did the family in which Adele grew up stop and the family she and John created begin? When the issue of loyalty emerged, the rule in her parents' family was so strong that the boundaries began to fade. As a result, she believed that if she lived closer, her mother would consume her attention, leaving her no time for John, their children, or herself. She convinced herself that only distance saved her from her sisters' fate, and that moving closer to her parents meant foregoing her life goals.

Therapist: Adele, what's it like for you when you hear John say, "If the kids and I want something that doesn't fit with what your parents want, too bad for us"?

Adele: Well, first I get furious. How can he accuse me of not caring about what he and the kids want, when I've spent so much time and energy taking care of them and giving them what they want? And then I wonder if maybe he's right. I really start doubting myself. Am I a grown-up? Am I my mother's puppet, like my sisters? But, I think, how could that be? I've worked so hard to be different and to behave differently, and to limit the time I spend with them. So, when I ask for time with them, I get pretty angry when John protests.

John: But you don't even like spending time with them.

Therapist: Adele, when you ask for time with them, is that what you want?

Adele: Sometimes, I guess. But after we get there, they're usually so awful I start wondering, what was I thinking?

Therapist: How would John know when you were asking for time you wanted to spend with them and when you were asking because you felt pressured?

Adele: I don't know. I guess I'd have to tell him. But sometimes I'm not even sure I know.

Therapist: It sounds like the pressure from both sides gets terribly confusing. But, it also seems so sad that at least sometimes you and John spend your vacations and holidays in a way neither of you prefers.

Examining boundary issues reveals how people feel compelled to do what they don't want to do. I'm not suggesting that Adele and John spend no time or feel no obligation to her parents. Rather, I'm suggesting that they plan, within the boundaries of their relationship, how often and under what conditions they will meet that obligation to her parents. Then, for example, they can convert the expectation that they join Adele's family for Christmas into an invitation to Adele's family to join them. Or, they can tell Adele's family that they are going on their summer vacation alone with the children but will visit over the long Labor Day or Memorial Day weekend.

Pete and Shelly: Drifting Apart

Pete was a reserved, 31-year-old engineer. Although his career would move forward quickly were he willing to work with clients, he chose to remain on the sidelines. Shelly, 35, was a teacher. She appeared warm and open and said she loved working with children and their parents.

Friends introduced Pete and Shelly five years ago. They married a couple of years later; and, for the past year, Shelly had been pressing Pete to have a child. She was concerned about her age and believed they had been together long enough to commit to becoming parents. She thought they had agreed to have children and was confused by Pete's reluctance. To complicate their situation, Pete's father had died six months previously. Shelly believed that Pete had begun to withdraw emotionally after she began pushing for a baby and then had withdrawn completely after his father died. The more quiet and hesitant Pete became, the more Shelly wondered about their future together.

Pete grew up in a family where depression was rampant. His mother had medicated herself with alcohol and prescription drugs. His father had withdrawn into silence. Pete considered his own moods stable. He enjoyed being with people and rarely drank any alcohol at all. Although he appeared reserved about himself, he enjoyed talking about movies, work, sports, politics, and boat building.

Pete said he'd never been much of a talker and didn't notice any difference. Shelly disagreed.

Shelly: I've always wanted him to talk more about himself, especially about his feelings. But at least he used to talk. Now, he barely says hello before disappearing into some project or book or television program. He doesn't even talk about work anymore. And when I plan something with friends, he tells me at the last minute he doesn't feel like going.

Pete: I think what Shelly says is an exaggeration. Maybe once or twice I haven't felt like doing something she's planned. But mostly, I don't think things have changed since we've gotten married. And they certainly haven't changed since my father died. This is who I am, the guy she married.

Shelly reiterated that she was worried that Pete was becoming withdrawn in the way his father had been.

Shelly: At family gatherings, even on holidays like Christmas, Frank [Pete's father] just sat there. Not smiling, not joining in. He looked like a robot going through the motions. And Mary [Pete's mother] would yell at him, call him names like "Party Pooper" and "Tin Man". When she drinks, she's so juvenile and mean. And he didn't respond. You wouldn't even know he'd heard her, except he'd look at her with such a sad expression on his face. If he'd looked mad, I wouldn't have thought it odd that he didn't say anything; after all, she'd been drinking for years, and he might have given up making a fuss about it every time. But, he looked like he somehow took it in. Or maybe he was just sad that he was married to her. Anyway, I think in all the years I knew him, I had one real conversation with him beyond the pleasantries of arriving and leaving. He didn't seem to enjoy life. Pete enjoys life, but only when he's alone, and I'm worried he's on a slippery slope and will become like his father, a misery to himself and everyone around him. And I don't want to bring a child into that. I don't even want to be in it myself sometimes.

Shelly said she'd tried everything she could think of to help Pete deal with his father's death and change back into who he'd been. She was cheerful, worked hard to reduce the stress in his home life, gave him reading material about bereavement and depression, and suggested he talk to a counselor. Finally, she called their family doctor to talk about her concerns. Pete was largely unresponsive, claiming he was fine and she didn't need to worry, he wasn't about to become like either of his parents. He seemed neither angry nor relieved that she'd talked to their physician or that they'd presented for therapy. Similarly, he'd ignored the books and articles about depression and bereavement Shelly had given him.

After exhausting her list of fix-its for closeness in her relationship with Pete, Shelly began to give up. She said she still wanted the relationship to work, but she was not hopeful. She concluded she needed to put off the decision about having a baby until after she determined what she was going to do about the relationship.

Meanwhile, she had been confiding her upset about Pete to her friends. These included a man she worked with, had always found attractive, but kept in the box marked "friend." As her hope for the future of her marriage receded, so did the edges of the box.

Shelly: This man seems to really understand me. He listens, he talks about his own relationships, and he even talks about feelings. I'm not sure Pete ever did. And it's nice, you know. But, he's not a threat to my marriage or anything. It's just nice for me to have a male perspective, and this man seems happy to talk to me.

Therapist: You sound surprised.

Shelly: Well, I guess I am. Pete hasn't seemed happy to talk to me in a long, long time, and I'm just realizing I've been wondering whether it's me he doesn't want to talk to, or him who doesn't want to talk. Do you know what I mean?

Therapist: It sounds like you've wondered whether Pete is depressed or just doesn't care about you anymore.

Shelly: Yes.

The fight in Pete and Shelly's relationship includes issues of intimacy, caring, trust, and loyalty. Let's examine these issues one at a time.

Intimacy. Shelly had also grown up in a silent and distant family. She longed for closeness. While she had wished Pete talked more about himself, she had been content with their level of intimacy before they began talking about children and his father died.

Shelly: He used to talk to me, about work and other things. But now he doesn't even do that. And we spend so little time together that it hardly feels like we're married. More like roommates. We don't do things together. We don't talk much to each other. And I don't feel close to him anymore.

Talking about oneself was part of Shelly's definition of intimacy. Many heterosexual women view emotional intimacy in terms of talking about feelings and about the relationship and discover their partners have no idea how to translate their requests into behavior. "I don't know what you want" becomes a familiar male refrain when faced with requests for emotional intimacy. While women tend to hear their partners' talk about work and activities as informative but not intimate, their male partners view these conversations as an indication of emotional closeness (13). More recent research has indicated biological gender differences linked to the role of testosterone in brain development (14) and communication (15).

Shelly said she'd be content to return to their previous level of emotional intimacy, even though she enjoyed her conversations with her male friend at work. Unfortunately, Pete didn't acknowledge the changes Shelly claimed and concluded there was no need for him to change the content or frequency with which he talked to her.

Having a life partner with whom to share experiences, joys, and difficulties was also important to Shelly. Irrespective of whose view of the relationship was more accurate, her unhappiness with Pete's behavior when they were at home and the level of his participation with her in social events led Shelly to view their relationship as two people sharing a house, rather than a life, together.

> Shelly: When I think about being married, I think about how we used to live. When we got home, we'd talk about our days with each other, help each other cook or clean up dinner, or go out together. And, sometimes we'd do things with friends and then talk about what we did and what our friends were up to. I really miss having Pete in my life in these ways.

> Pete: I'm not sure we ever spent as much time together as you remember.

Caring. *The* fight about caring was simple: Shelly perceived Pete withdrawing and interpreted it as an indication he no longer cared about her. Although she knew his behavior was about pressure and grief and had nothing to do with his feelings about her, on another level Pete's withdrawal felt personal.

Shelly: It feels like he doesn't care anymore. I say things like, I'm worried he's turning into his father. But I also think he's pulling away and it feels like, if he really cared, he wouldn't be doing this. If he loved me and cared about me like he used to, he'd still want us to be doing things together.

Pete: As I've said, I don't think we ever spent as much time together as you seem to remember. But, I don't want to argue about it. The point is I do still care about you. I just don't have time do a lot with you right now. And, I don't feel like a big social life with other people, either. I could argue that if you cared about me, you'd stop pestering me to do things I don't want to do and criticizing me for needing time to myself.

Pete and Shelly obviously disagreed about how to show caring. Each demonstrated caring in the way s/he would like caring shown. Shelly wanted Pete to express caring by spending more time with her, both alone at home and socially; she let him know this by asking him to do things with her and telling him about her upset when he didn't. Pete, on the other hand, wanted Shelly to demonstrate caring by not pushing him to interact with her or their friends. He therefore left Shelly alone to do whatever interested her, as he himself would have liked to be left alone.

Trust and Loyalty. When the status quo is tolerable, even if just barely so, the situation must worsen in order to activate a couple to change. Thus, an emotionally close relationship like the one Shelly had with her male colleague sometimes must develop into a physically close relationship in order for a couple to realize the severity of their situation and also how much they want to remain together.

One view of suicide gestures, and even some suicide attempts, is that they are cries for help. If Shelly's emotionally intimate relationship with her male friend became physically intimate, it would be as though she and Pete covertly appointed her to make a relationship suicide gesture. Their previous status quo of increasing distance would then cross the line from tolerable to intolerable, leaving them no alternative but to change.

Allowing the status quo to continue until an affair occurs usually creates negative consequences as well. While it forces a couple to seek ways to change their negative interactions, it disrupts trust and calls into question the straying partner's loyalty to the betrayed partner and to the relationship. As a consequence, attempts by either partner to rebuild trust and a sense of loyalty to one another can turn into *the* fight about trust and/or loyalty.

When Shelly eventually engaged in a physical affair with her friend at work, three issues arose: Shelly's loyalty to her marriage to Pete; Pete's importance to her; and whether Pete could trust her to end the affair and not have another one sometime in the future. These are typical components of *the* fight about trust and loyalty following an affair.

> Pete: You say you don't think I care about you, that you're not important enough to me, because I don't spend more time with you. *But, what about you?* Did you think of me at all while you were with him? Were my feelings important to you then? You want me to believe you care about me and you want to be married to me. What, besides your words, would lead me to believe either?

Like any couple struggling with an affair, Pete and Shelly were at a critical point in their relationship. While the potential to change was great, the potential for *the* fight about trust and loyalty to spiral out of control and lead to the break-up of their relationship was also great.

There were several warning signals of an impending affair in Shelly's story. First, she was giving up. Second, she said she didn't feel close to Pete anymore. And, finally, she was confiding in friends about both. While many women talk to their friends about their relationships, talking about hopelessness often breeds more hopelessness. Consider a friend's empathy: "It sounds awful." "You must feel so lonely." "There's nothing worse than feeling lonely when you're not alone." "Think how stuck you'd feel if you had kids." All would be well meaning. All would indicate that Shelly's friends cared about her. And all of these statements tell her she's right, her relationship with Pete is awful and thus would inadvertently lead her toward the door out of the relationship, rather than toward a resolution of *the* fight about trust, loyalty, caring, or intimacy.

Serena and Brad: Never Together

Serena and Brad had just celebrated their 40th birthdays. Both were intense individuals who liked to see themselves as more mellow than they really were.

They had met in their mid-20s and were instantly attracted to one another. Their relationship was filled with passion, and both believed they were soul mates destined to be together. However, neither could remember anything they talked about or did together that wasn't romantic.

During the 16 years since their relationship began, Serena and Brad had been separated three times. Serena initiated the first two, Brad the third.

At the time of the first separation, Serena had been unsure whether she was ready for a permanent commitment and wondered whether her uncertainty reflected a flaw in her relationship with Brad. She had dated a couple of people during the separation and had decided dating was too meaningless after her relationship with Brad. Brad had not dated; rather, he had remained certain that he and Serena would reconcile. When they did, they decided to put the separation behind them and immediately set a date for their wedding. At the time, both were convinced that Serena's fear of a relationship flaw had been a predictable case of jitters and nothing more. Wedding plans then consumed their time and conversations.

Their second separation occurred five years later. Serena had again raised the issue of a flaw in the relationship. After several months apart, she realized she loved Brad and wanted to be with him, so they again reconciled. Brad had remained confident that Serena would return. However, he had been angry with her for leaving again and had dated during this separation.

Again, following the second separation, Brad and Serena reconciled without considering what Serena meant by "flaw." They were relieved and happy to be together again. Both were concerned they would undermine their reunion by discussing the problems and chose to wait until the relationship felt more stable. And, of course, when things between them were going well, they felt no need to discuss what felt like an old, rather than a current, problem.

The third separation occurred seven years later. Serena had been feeling dissatisfied with her career, pressured by her age to decide about having a family, and bored with her routine. But this time she decided that the problem resided in her and resolved to stay in the relationship. Meanwhile, Brad was also feeling dissatisfied with their life together and pressured by Serena to decide about children. He wondered if, perhaps, Serena wasn't the right woman for him. He decided he hadn't paid attention to his own concerns about her but rather had been preoccupied with her ambivalence. The idea of living alone and not answering to her expectations became more and more appealing. He told her all this and moved out.

The third separation lasted 6 months. Serena initially surprised herself by how devastated she felt. After 3 or 4 months of misery, however, she found she enjoyed being on her own. She changed jobs, spent lots of time with friends, ate popcorn for dinner, and adopted a cat.

Brad also changed jobs. In addition, he joined a gym and dated. He saw Serena occasionally during the first few months of this separation, but as she began to feel better she became less available. By the end of the fifth month, Brad was beginning to miss her and started thinking that his personal life seemed shallow and unfulfilling. He approached Serena, who said she was open to the idea of reconciling but was concerned about the risk of failure. She worried that Brad might decide to leave again, and she didn't want to repeat what the first few months of this separation had been like. Eventually, he convinced her that he'd just needed to get whatever this had been out of his system, as she had during their previous separations. They reconciled, each believing their separations had been about whoever left and not about their relationship. Six months later, Serena became pregnant.

Two years after that, with a fifteen-month-old child, Brad again wondered whether he'd been happier apart from Serena. He decided she'd been correct, that the relationship was flawed. He believed their relationship held them both back from being as fulfilled as they could be, and that they were both happier away from each other. He believed that his love for Serena had caused him to reconcile with her against his better judgment in the past, and the time had come to exert his reason over his emotions. He also convinced himself that their son would be happier with parents who divorced before he could remember them living as a family.

Brad was aware that moving out again would probably be an irreversible decision and so hesitated to make it. He became quiet and contemplative and stopped telling Serena how much he loved her and their life together. Serena, noticing the change, announced that she thought they should have another baby.

Several things could have happened to Brad and Serena's relationship at this point: Brad could have had an affair; Serena could have gotten pregnant again; Brad could have announced that the last reconciliation was a mistake and left; or all three could have happened at the same time. Then they could each have hired lawyers, or they could have gone another round of separation and reconciliation. In any case, the pattern was already clear: Serena and Brad were both committed to their relationship but were unable to sustain this commitment simultaneously.

The fight in Brad and Serena's relationship illustrated themes of distance regulation, relationship contract, and power. Like the first three couples, their relationship also exemplified how trash turns into garbage.

Distance Regulation. Brad and Serena's rocky history can be viewed from the perspective that, as long as one or the other questioned the relationship, they were able to maintain a comfortable distance between them. When they felt uncomfortably close, one of them left. When the ensuing distance became too great, the one who left suggested reconciling. This phenomenon exemplifies the parable of Schopenhauer's porcupines, in which porcupines must find a balance between the pain of encountering one another's quills when they get too close and yet huddling close enough together for warmth (16).

Serena and Brad's pattern of separation and reconciliation suggested greater comfort with at least one of their combined four feet out the door than with one leaving irrevocably or both committing whole-heartedly. Their periodic separations precluded the emotional closeness they both described when talking about how, upon meeting, they had felt they were soul mates but that had become overwhelming. On the other hand, the ensuing reconciliations kept the relationship from unraveling altogether. Unfortunately, this pattern of regulating distance also made them unhappy.

So, as a couple, Brad and Serena failed to find a stable level of distance. Instead, they found themselves stuck in this cycle of separation and reconciliation. On a pragmatic level, being together and its resultant closeness left them feeling confined, restless, and doubtful about the relationship. Separation, on the other hand, led them to remember how much they wanted to be together, and then they reconciled.

> Therapist: I'm curious what the connection is between feeling confined by your relationship and wondering whether it's flawed?
>
> Serena: I'm not sure. Maybe the first time I was feeling a little bored. Maybe the second time, too.
>
> Brad: I wouldn't say confined or bored. I'd say she's flaky, probably has a commitment problem.
>
> Serena: Commitment problem? After you want to walk out on fatherhood? Give me a break.
>
> Brad: It's a lot more complicated than that. You've never listened to my concerns.
>
> Serena: Only because I was afraid talking about them would drive you away again.
>
> Therapist: From this and other things you've told me, it sounds like talking about your relationship feels very risky.
>
> Serena: Well, we *should* be able to talk about our relationship. Don't you think there's something wrong that we can't?
>
> Therapist: I don't think avoiding talking about it has helped. But if it feels risky, it's understandable that you haven't wanted to talk about it. I also wonder how close you'd feel to each other if you did talk about it.
>
> Brad: Yeah, right Serena. You think we should talk about it but all you do is get all mushy and babble about how great things are between us.

And jumping ahead:

> Therapist: What about before you get back together? It sounds like you miss each other. Would it be fair to say you feel too close together just before you separate and too far apart after you've been separated for a while?
>
> Serena: I guess that's one way of looking at it.
>
> Brad: Yeah, maybe. It feels like there's something wrong when we're together, but then when we're apart we kind of decide it's not so important. And we miss each other. So we get back together. Don't you think that's what happens, Serena?
>
> Serena: Yes, I guess so.

<u>Relationship contract</u>. Two covert clauses in the relationship contract adversely affected Brad and Serena. The first entailed the expectation that they would never question being together. Many couples hold the ideas that when two people are in love they always want to be together and that good relationships require no effort, and then equate questions or difficulties with flaws. Brad and Serena covertly agreed that they would not question their relationship or acknowledge problems, and, if questions or problems arose anyway, they would terminate the relationship.

> Therapist: What does each of you expect from a partner?
>
> Serena: I don't know.
>
> Therapist: Brad?
>
> Brad: I expected that if the relationship was right for us we'd stay together and if it wasn't we'd split up. I didn't expect all this waffling back and forth. I thought we'd just know whether we belonged together or not.

The second problematic clause in their relationship contract involved the expectation that each would make the other happy, irrespective of what else was happening in their lives. This clause led both Brad and Serena to define personal unhappiness as a sign of problems between them. They would look inside themselves for the source of their unhappiness only after a separation, when the distance between them had become intolerable and the other one wasn't there to blame.

> Therapist: So, Serena, any ideas about your expectations for relationships?
>
> Serena: I thought we'd be happy together, that being together would make up for other problems in our lives, like at work. And I thought we'd have children.
>
> Brad: Yeah, I agree with Serena. Being together should be enough, even if life outside the relationship is difficult.

As will become apparent in Chapters 6 and 7, these assumptions, or clauses in a relationship contract, must be questioned. No relationship could survive the pressures to fix difficulties in one's partner's life and to be always happy. These expectations, embedded in the relationship contract, contributed to *the* fight in Brad and Serena's relationship.

Power. Brad and Serena's distance regulation struggle contained a power component. Specifically, who decided whether they separated had power over the other. And Brad and Serena fought about who held this power.

To exemplify *the* fight about power in their relationship, let's go back to the beginning of the previous therapy excerpt and create an alternative ending.

> Therapist: I'm curious what the connection is between feeling confined by your relationship and wondering whether it's flawed?

Serena: I'm not sure. Maybe the first time I was feeling a little bored. Maybe the second time, too. Of course, I can't say about the last time, since that was Brad's idea.

Brad: Oh, it's my fault? Like, you're just the perfect, happy little wife and suddenly old flaky Brad decides to bolt? Sounds more like you, Babe.

Serena: Excuse me, Brad, but it seems to me fatherhood was maybe a little too much for you.

Even as they agreed that the pattern of separation and reconciliation maintained a necessary though uncomfortable regulation of distance in their relationship, Brad and Serena argued about who had the power to distribute responsibility for this distance between them. They appeared to be saying, "It's ok if I choose to separate, but if you do you're being flaky," i.e., I but not you have the power to decide whether we stay together.

Brad and Serena's history also demonstrated how trash turns into garbage. By not examining their relationship following their separations, Brad and Serena avoided looking at the problems between them. The problems, therefore, remained unresolved. Additionally, each time they attempted to solve their problems by separating, the separation created additional sources of distress and conflict between them, including anger at the one who seized power and initiated the separation. In other words, separating increased the garbage in their relationship. Separations and the ensuing garbage did not help this couple arrive at shared values about being partners or a comfortable distance within their relationship. Nor did these separations allow them to resolve their power or distance regulation issues. Rather, the separations added to their questions about their relationship, the distance they need between them, and who had the power to decide whether they would be together.

In order for Brad and Serena to avoid ending their relationship, someone also had to decide to reconcile. As with their separations, garbage accumulated about who and how that partner was granted the power to decide. Their history suggests that only the one who left had the power to decide to reconcile, as in none of the three instances did the one who was left initiate reconciliation.

Conclusion

We will revisit these four couples again in Chapters 5 and 7. In Chapter 5, I will describe how these couples identified *the* fights within their relationships. In Chapter 7, I will elaborate on what they did to resolve *the* fights and get rid of the garbage, including both what worked and what was unsuccessful.

Part II
Identifying the Source of Your Garbage

4

Identifying *the* Fight

Identifying *the* fight in your relationship is the first step toward resolving it. You cannot resolve something until you know what it is. But learning to recognize *the* fight, what precipitates it, and how it affects each of you is not as simple as it sounds.

You may have read things that sounded very familiar to you in earlier chapters. However, you need to apply them to your situation in very specific ways as a first step toward changing what is bothering you about your relationship. And, again, the first step toward change is recognition, or identification; because, if you don't know what it is you wish to change, you cannot change it.

There may be any number of ways to identify *the* fight in your relationship. When I work with couples, I find it helpful to view assessment, or identification of *the* fight, as a series of ongoing, or working, scientific hypotheses. As I try different approaches to help couples resolve their fights, I modify my hypotheses to fit the feedback the couple provides. In this chapter, I am going to take you through a similar method for identifying *the* fight in your own relationship and developing working hypotheses to guide you through the process of resolving it.

You are undoubtedly one of the two greatest experts about what it's like to live in your relationship. You may know, like all of the couples you've read about so far, that certain attitudes and behaviors of your partner's infuriate or sadden you. Like the couples in Chapter 3, you may even know that your relationship is causing you great pain.

To identify *the* fight in your relationship, you now need to become a scientific expert about your relationship. Emotions offer terrific clues to what's wrong, but by themselves they won't provide you with enough information to guide you in changing it. So, you're going to add to the expertise you already have, not replace it.

To begin the process of becoming a scientific expert about your relationship, you are going to read a quick review of the scientific method, which we will be using throughout this chapter. Then, I'll provide you with some techniques for studying your relationship. We're going to approach your relationship in the way anthropologists and, more recently, some sociologists and psychologists approach the study of small groups and cultures with which they are not familiar. I think it's also how therapists approach their work with clients. Specifically, we'll observe, identify patterns, hypothesize about how these patterns arise and how you and your partner respond, test the hypotheses, revise them, and, in Part III, explore a range of possible solutions.

I know it's tempting to skip directly to Part III and begin enacting those solutions. Please remember that no solution to anything as complex as a relationship can possibly be a one-size-fits-all model. In other words, solutions likely will not work unless they are tailored to the way a particular issue plays out in your relationship.

You'll begin by examining your arguments, disagreements, discussions, and fights—whatever word for these incidents you are most comfortable using—with your partner, if possible. These are what I've been calling trash. Your goal is to identify evidence of *the* fight in your relationship, as it appears in these situations. Your ultimate goal is to resolve *the* fight, so that these episodes remain just trash, rather than generating new garbage in your relationship.

The Scientific Method

Do you remember memorizing the four steps of the scientific method in middle school, or junior high? Neither do I. So, to refresh us both, they are:

- Generating hypotheses about *the* fight in your relationship;

- Gathering data about *the* fight in your relationship;

- Analyzing the data about *the* fight in your relationship;

- Drawing conclusions about your hypotheses from the data analysis.

In this chapter, we are going to observe arguments in your relationship which lead to *the* fight, identify any patterns displayed in these arguments, hypothesize about how these patterns arise and how you and your partner respond, test the hypotheses by gathering and analyzing data about those arguments which lead to *the* fight, revise the hypotheses, and draw conclusions. In Chapter 6, we will use your conclusions to help you find ways to resolve *the* fight in your relationship and thus stop generating new garbage.

If your partner is willing to do these exercises with you, the benefits will be enormous. You can work together on the exercises, or you and your partner can each do the exercises separately and then compare your findings. Working together to identify *the* fight in your relationship helps make the process easier. Working together also helps illuminate each of your contributions and responses to *the* fight. Together, you will find it easier to clarify how your reactions to each other exacerbate *the* fight in your relationship.

One partner (you) may be much more enthusiastic about undertaking this endeavor than the other. Or, it may be difficult for the two of you to collaborate at all at this point in your relationship. If it's not feasible to work together on this project, for any reason, you will be left to speculate about your partner. Also, without input from your partner, it may be difficult to move outside your own view of the situation, so what you see may be skewed. For example, you may find that your partner looks like a jerk, while you are the victim of her or his endless rage. If you are working alone, and you notice that one of you looks great on paper while the other looks like someone even a saint couldn't live with, stop and ask yourself what you're missing, both about yourself and about your partner. If your answer is nothing, then ask yourself what you are doing in the situation in which you find yourself.

Generating Hypotheses

A hypothesis is a research question. We are interested in two very general_research questions.

- What is *the* fight about?

- What triggers *the* fight in your relationship?

You will also need to ask yourself more specific questions about each.

Before you start, get yourself some kind of notebook to write in. It can be a scientific notebook, a beautiful journal, or a spiral-lined pad. It can also be some scratch paper that you keep in a used envelope or folder. The choice is yours. None works better than another.

Perhaps you'd prefer something that makes a more formal statement about your commitment to the project you're undertaking. If you are saying to yourself, "I've never been able to keep a journal," you may find it easier if the journal is very informal. Less formal journals are not so intimidating, and so you may not feel so pressured to write neatly or well.

Consider whether you'd like to have it always available. If so, be sure it's something small that will fit in your briefcase or purse.

Cost, of course, is also an issue. The important point is that the notebook is a tool, so find a tool that will help make this task manageable for you.

You met Samantha and Alan in Chapter 3. I'm going to use brief examples from their notebooks throughout this chapter to illustrate their use. Notice as you read the examples not only how they illustrate Samantha and Alan's use of their notebooks but also how differently each views the same argument. It's not easy to discern what is going on between them solely from one or the other's perspective. That's why I recommended you do these exercises with your partner, if at all possible.

The first way to generate questions is to examine theory and previous research. Your previous research includes your life experiences, your experiences with your partner, and what you've read. Did any of the nine issues described in Chapter 2 or the four couples introduced in Chapter 3 resonate with your experience of your relationship? Have you read other self-help books that have described a dynamic that seemed true for you? Have you been in individual or couple counseling, and did the therapist say anything that struck you as true about yourself or the dynamics of your relationship? What do you know about yourself and your partner as individuals that might influence how you act in a conflict situation? If you're not sure, ask a trusted friend or family member (though not a child because the question might lead her/him to feel s/he needs to take sides) what they've noticed about you and conflict, your partner and conflict, or even better, the two of you together.

Create a list of what you learn as you answer these questions, and write it in your notebook. Label the list, "Previous Research". You may add to this list at any time, even after you've finished generating hypotheses.

You may need to elaborate on your previous research. Look at the list you've made from other sources—Chapters 2 and 3, other self-help books, therapists, and family or friends—and ask yourself whether any of the items on the list needs to be more precise. If an item has given you a clue but the clue seems vague or undeveloped to you, take some time to elaborate or modify it.

For example, you may believe that emotional intimacy is an issue in your marriage and resonate with the idea that you don't get enough support. In Chapter 2, while describing the theme of intimacy, I suggested that you ask specifically for what you want, since the word "support" can be confusing or misleading. The concept of asking specifically for what you want or saying exactly what you intend to convey could be applied to a wide range of situations. If your list includes a note that asking for "support" or anything else is incredibly difficult for you and that you'd rather do it yourself than ask for help, the words "support" and "anything" may need clarification. For you, then, being specific about what you want from your partner means overcoming your reluctance to ask in addition to the challenge of being specific about what you want.

Similarly, you may have discovered or read something that describes you pretty well, but not exactly. Write your own observations on the list also. For example, if a friend says, "Betsy, you don't seem to like conflict. I can't imagine you starting a fight" and you know that your partner sometimes so infuriates you that you needle him until he starts the fight; the notion that you dislike conflict so much that you won't start a fight may need elaboration. Write: "My friend thinks I do not like conflict and won't start it; I know I push my partner into starting an argument when I'm angry and won't start the argument myself." It's an important dynamic in your relationship that your partner agrees to be the "bad guy" and start the fights, even when it's you who's angry.

The second way to generate hypotheses is from observations. You will need to observe both yourself and your interactions with your partner. If you are working on this project alone, you will need to move outside yourself and observe your interactions with your partner as someone else would. This is incredibly difficult. If you are able to take your partner's perspective, even if you are only guessing what it might be, you are on the way toward a shift from being stuck with your own outlook as the only viewpoint to empathizing with your partner's point of view.

To observe yourself, begin by examining your feelings. Ask yourself what they are, when you feel them, what else is going on when you feel them, and how you react to them.

Make a list of your feelings in a section of your notebook called, "Feelings". Include all your feelings, both positive and negative. Note the time of day and day of the week when you notice your feelings. Also keep track of what else is going on when your feelings arise. Pay particular attention to what your partner is doing at the time: is s/he avoiding you, distracting you, doing whatever it is s/he does that makes you uncomfortable? Finally, note how you handle these feelings. Do you stuff them inside and then become anxious or angry? Does your stomach churn or your neck hurt? If you change your behavior toward your partner in any way as a result of these feelings, such as becoming tense or saying something sarcastic, write it down.

It might be helpful to record your feelings. Seeing them on paper will allow you to become more specific about what they are and when they arise.

Next, observe your interactions with your partner. Be especially alert to your trash, or incidents of anger, frustration, arguments—again, whatever word you find most comfortable to describe conflict with your partner. You can pick a number, say 3 or 4 arguments, or you can observe every argument that occurs over a particular time period, say the next 2-4 weeks. Keep a record of all of your observations in your notebook, and label them, "Preliminary Observations".

As with your "Previous Research" section, you can add additional observations to either your "Feelings" or "Preliminary Observations" at any time. Whatever you think and observe about yourself and your relationship may be helpful, so don't worry about when you thought or noticed it.

As soon as possible after an argument or fight, write down as much of what happened as you can remember. Especially important are: voice tone, body language, how you felt while you were talking, how you felt while your partner was talking, as close an approximation as you can record to what was said, and the order in which it was said.

Examine what you have written about your argument. Then ask yourself these four questions:

- When did the argument shift from whatever triggered it to accusations, criticisms, or other topics?
- How did it shift (words, nonverbal communications)?
- Who shifted it?
- What happened just before it shifted? What happened after it shifted?

This is the crucial point in the argument, because at this point the argument probably began the process of becoming *the* fight. Write down the answers to these questions, either after your description of the argument or in margins you've left alongside the description.

The first couple in Chapter 3, Samantha and Alan, provide a wonderful example of what happened as an argument shifted into *the* fight. Their argument was about a chores schedule for the children. I'll repeat it here with my own comments about how they moved from the argument to *the* fight.

> Samantha: This is an opportunity for us to work together, like we used to, and develop a chores schedule and a way of enforcing it that works for our family.

> Alan: That's a smokescreen, Sam. [Ticking off on the fingers of one hand with the index finger of the other] You're disorganized, you've opposed a chores schedule in the past, and now you're trying to get me to create one. Forget it. It's your job, not mine.

Right away, Alan moved the argument away from the chores schedule to their power issue, by shifting to the question of whose job it was to prepare a chores schedule. He also attacked Samantha and probably made her feel pretty defensive. Finally, he brought up the garbage generated by previous episodes of *the* fight, by reminding Samantha that she'd opposed a chores schedule in the past, thus supporting his attack about her wanting him to take it on now and his criticism about her lack of organization. He also shifted what Samantha posed as a joint task into a choice between it being his or her responsibility. He didn't allow the possibility of it being neither his nor hers but a shared task; sharing it was immediately ruled out as an option.

> Samantha: It [chores schedule] won't work unless the kids know we're both committed to it.

Samantha returned to the argument about a chores schedule. However, she also allowed herself to be drawn into *the* fight about who decides who's responsible for getting the kids to do their chores. This may have been inevitable. In Chapter 6, I'll describe some possibilities for derailing *the* fight by recognizing and addressing its presence. Here, Alan and Samantha continued *the* fight without acknowledging it, leaving them little hope of resolving it during this discussion.

> Alan: I didn't say I wasn't committed to it [chores schedule]. I just said it's your job to create and enforce it. If I have to, I'll back you up.

Alan continued to insist they move away from the trash of the chores schedule into *the* fight about their power issue.

> Samantha: Why is it that you get to decide whose job it is? I think it's *our* job as a couple.

This time, Samantha followed him into *the* fight and addressed it more or less directly, by reminding him that she viewed the chores schedule as a joint task, rather than either his or hers alone.

> Alan: No, not since you stopped working.

Now he added their issues about their relationship contract and the no-longer-shared value about what a good partner does to the argument about power. He accurately assessed these three themes becoming intertwined as they turn into *the* fight for him and Samantha.

> Samantha: If I'd stopped working altogether like I wanted to, then we might talk about my taking all the responsibility for this.

> Alan: Oh, please. This is ancient history, and I don't have time for it this morning.

At this point, the chores schedule was forgotten and therefore the argument about it couldn't be resolved. As a result, rather than an opportunity to resolve *the* fight, this argument became more garbage and will likely reappear in future iterations of *the* fight.

The processes of previous research and preliminary observation of the argument described above have led to an hypothesis regarding *the* fight in Alan and Samantha's relationship: *the* fight is about whether and how much Samantha works outside the home and includes the three issues of power, relationship contract, and shared values.

It's also reasonable to hypothesize that Alan and Samantha discussing anything related to how much she works outside the home precipitates *the* fight. In this instance, asking Alan to participate in creating a chores schedule appears to have triggered his anger about Samantha not continuing to work full-time outside the home. And once his anger emerged, Samantha remembered her own anger about his insistence that she continue to work outside the home at all. And once they became angry, each one's anger escalated in response to the other's angry statements.

But this dynamic only portrays half of the picture. I suspect Samantha also sometimes became angry at Alan about the time she spent away from her children and at work. Her anger may then have emerged in her requests for help or otherwise been expressed nonverbally. And when these requests and/or nonverbal messages angered Alan, she may have already been fuming.

Every time either was reminded about her work outside the home, Samantha and Alan had *the* fight about it all over again. And, it seems logical to hypothesize that, since neither *the* fight nor the topics which precipitated it got resolved, new garbage arose with each repetition of *the* fight about whether and how much Samantha works outside the home.

After you've recorded what you've learned from other sources (previous research) and a detailed description of your feelings and some of your arguments (preliminary observations), you'll be ready to write specific answers to the two questions: what is *the* fight about and what triggers it? As you work to develop your hypotheses, you may find that these two questions turn into a number of more precise questions. Feel free to generate new questions and as many hypotheses as cross your mind; brainstorm as much as possible. And don't worry about whether you've got too many or too few, or even whether you're repeating yourself. You can edit them later. Write these questions and/or hypotheses in your notebook under the heading, "Research Questions" or "Hypotheses," whichever you'd prefer.

These are your hypotheses, the first step in your scientific quest. Based on your preliminary research and preliminary observations you now know enough to make an educated guess about what *the* fight in your relationship might be and how it begins and continues once it's started. All scientists need their questions, or hypotheses, to be as specific as possible. Your questions, or hypotheses, about *the* fight in your relationship must be specific to your own situation to be useful to you.

Here is a sample of the hypothesis generating section of Samantha and Alan's notebooks. Yours need not look like this, but it's a template to use if you need one, as well as an illustration of how to use your notebook. I've added some comments to help you think about your own recordings.

Samantha and Alan have decided to keep separate notebooks and then compare them later. The entries from their notebooks are bulleted and my comments are inserted below their entries.

Please remember that I'm only describing a small portion of their notebooks. You'll need to observe at least three or four of your own interactions with your partner in order to generate enough details to understand your patterns.

Samantha's Notebook

The Fight with Alan

Previous Research

- Kathy [their previous couple therapist] said we needed to spend more time together and talk about our shared goals; it helped when we did that, but we stopped after we stopped seeing her.
- Lucy [Samantha's previous therapist] said I have trouble asking for what I need.
- I think maybe I let Alan start our fights.

Preliminary Observations

Feelings:

- I am lonely and angry because Alan doesn't want to spend time with me and isn't very nice when we are together. I feel rejected.
- When I suggest we do something together and Alan says no, I feel hurt and rejected.
- When Alan's being unfair, not recognizing how hard I work at home and at the office and how much I want to be home with the kids, I get really, really angry at him.

Saturday, 2/2/02—11 am:

- Alan was finishing breakfast and reading the paper, and I thought it was a good time to talk about how to manage the kids' chores. He seemed pretty relaxed, and the kids weren't around to interrupt, so it seemed like a good time to have a serious conversation.

[Note: Samantha neglected to consider the impact of her feelings about Alan (she was upset that he'd slept late and was sitting around reading the paper when there was a lot to do) on the conversation she was about to start. It's very difficult to have a productive conversation when one person is already furious; the anger leaks through. If you are able to, notice the way in which your feelings about your partner show in your voice, body language, or even the words you choose. Your partner will notice, so if you're doing this together, you can also ask her/him.]

- I sat down at the table with him and said, "Honey, let's talk about a chores schedule for the kids. I'd like them to have regular chores and do them before they go out on Saturdays. Meagan says she keeps a chores schedule on her refrigerator and the kids check off what they've done." I think my voice was upbeat and I was smiling.

[Note: I can't imagine Alan missed her upset and tension, even if what he saw was as subtle as tightness around her mouth or a phoniness to her smile. If you find yourself trying to hide negative feelings, as Samantha was doing, ask yourself how your negative feelings may be manifested in your nonverbal behavior and whether your partner will assume from experience with you that you're not as upbeat as you portray yourself to be.]

- Without looking up from the paper, Alan said, "Fine, Samantha. Make a chores schedule." He sounded like he didn't want to be bothered.

[Note: What about his voice tone sounded like he didn't want to be bothered? There's a fine line between interpreting someone else's behavior and describing it, and the line is often difficult to see. I'm not sure which Samantha is doing here; it sounds like interpretation. I'd like to know whether his voice was flat (no inflection), condescending, unusually loud or soft, or something else.]

- I was angry that he wouldn't look at me. I thought, maybe he missed my point, so I said, "This is an opportunity for us to work together for our family." My voice probably sounded whiny or edgy.

[Note: This isn't verbatim from the dialogue presented in either Chapter 3 or earlier in this chapter. It's unlikely anyone would accurately remember everything s/he said, so I'm making it shorter. It's also possible to remember what you intended to say, as well as what you said, and therefore write more in your notebook than you actually said.]

The words, "This is an opportunity for us to work together…" sound pleasant, but in a context in which Samantha is feeling more aggravated by Alan's response than she was when she brought up the subject of a chores schedule, I suspect that her voice tone was more consistent with her feelings than with her words. And, I suspect Alan heard the tone much louder than the words, and responded to it.]

- So, then he got mad. He said, "You're disorganized, and you've never helped me with getting the kids to do chores when I've tried. It's not my job to get the kids to do the chores. I won't help you." His voice was cold, critical, and accusing.

[Note: Alan didn't actually say he wouldn't help, but it was pretty clear he wasn't responding to Samantha's suggestion with enthusiasm or offers of cooperation. It is therefore not at all surprising that Samantha remembered his words as more negative than they were, especially since she heard a very negative voice tone and relationship message.]

- I was really mad that he'd accused me of being disorganized and uncooperative in the past. I don't remember that at all. I wanted to argue about it so he'd see I was right—I say that a lot, don't I? But, I also wanted to stick to the subject, so I said, "Getting the kids to do chores won't work unless they know we're both committed."

- So then he said in a voice that sounded like I was stupid or something, "I didn't say I wasn't committed to it. I just said it was your job. I'll back you up if I have to."
- I thought, thanks a lot for nothing. I was really disappointed. And hurt. And angry.
- I asked, "Why do you get to decide whose job it is?"
- He said, "It's your job because you don't work." He looked like he didn't like me.

[Note: Here's where the argument became *the* fight. Also, she does work, both in and outside the home.]

- I lost it. So I said, "I do too work. And I need some help around here. Maybe if I'd stayed home like I wanted to, it'd be different."
- He got up and said, "This is ancient history, Samantha. I'm going out." And he left.

My observations about this argument:

- We were really fighting about whose job it is from the beginning, even though I intended to talk about the kids' chores. I thought it was both our jobs and he thought it was mine. We got angrier as we went along.
- We started our same old fight about me working right after we began to fight about whether we make a chores schedule his way (my job) or mine (together).

Hypotheses:

- *The* most important fight in our marriage is about me not working full time after the children were born: I am still angry that I am working at all, and Alan is still angry that I didn't want to continue to work full time.

- When we talk about ourselves as a couple or family and Alan is reminded of how angry he is that I don't work full time, we have *the* fight.

[Note: Samantha's second hypothesis overlooked the point that when she's reminded of how angry she is that she's working outside the home at all, *the* fight also happens. In other words, it isn't just about Alan's anger. Additionally, "When we talk about ourselves as a couple or family" may be too general as an hypothesis.]

Alan's Notebook

The Fight w/Sam

Previous research:

- We've been in therapy and need to do more together.

Feelings:

- I'm frustrated with Sam because she's so involved with the kids. I miss her enthusiasm about her work.
- I'm tired of her nagging and anger.

Saturday, 2/2/02:

- I was reading the paper when Sam started talking about the kids' chores. She looked like she wanted to fight.

[Note: What was it about her look that left Alan believing she wanted to fight?]

- She said, "Help me make a chores schedule for the kids. My friend at work has one and we need one, too."
- I said, "Make it then."
- She didn't think a chores schedule was such a good idea when *I* wanted one.

[Note: He sounds hurt.]

- She said, "This is something we could do together."
- So then I told her that if she wanted to do more together, this wasn't it. I reminded her we'd already tried a chores schedule and she'd been too disorganized to make it work.
- She said we both had to make it, so I said, "You're it. I'll support you if the kids won't cooperate." I'm not going through this again.
- Then she said it isn't fair that I get to decide whether to help. I asked her where she got off telling me to do more and we started fighting about her damn job. She whines about working all the time and I'm sick of hearing about it. I told her, I've kept working and you don't hear *me* complaining about.

[Note: Alan is clearly furious and has honed in on *the* fight about Samantha working outside the home, which underlies the argument about the chores schedule. I wish he'd written more about his view of their nonverbal communications.]

Observations:

- Samantha doesn't miss an opportunity to remind me about what an ogre I am because she doesn't get to stay home all the time.

Hypotheses:

- *The* fight is about her changing after she had a baby and not wanting to work anymore.
- Sam can't talk to me any more without getting mad.

[Note: Like Samantha, Alan views *the* fight as about the other's anger while overlooking the impact of his own.]

Samantha and Alan both recognized that *the* fight in their relationship was about Samantha changing her mind about working full time outside the home after the birth of their first child. They also agreed that power was a factor in their decision-making.

A comparison of Samantha and Alan's notebooks also reveals some interesting differences in perspective. While there were similarities in how they remembered the argument, they differed in what aspects of it they viewed as important. They also saw their own and each others' roles in *the* fight very differently. A comparison of their notebooks reveals that each thought the other was angrier and more to blame. Additionally, each saw the other as having been more influential, or powerful, in Samantha's decision about working outside the home after they had children. And, finally, there is a clear difference in their enthusiasm for this journaling exercise, which reflects a common situation in which one partner (more often the woman in a heterosexual relationship) is more invested in examining the relationship than is the other.

It is always easier to see the other's role in *the* fight than one's own. So, be sure to ask yourself whether and how you may have contributed to the shift from an argument into *the* fight.

Although I want you to record more than one argument and hopefully more than a couple of hypotheses, these sample entries in Samantha and Alan's notebooks are enough to illustrate the generating hypotheses section of your notebook. I also want this exercise to be manageable for you, so do as much as you can while avoiding becoming too overwhelmed to continue. If the latter happens, take a break and return to your notebook later. Being overwhelmed may indicate that you've done enough observing and hypothesis generation for the time being. If this is the case, move on to the next section of this chapter.

Hypothesis Testing: Gathering Data

There are two reasons to test your hypotheses. First, you need to be sure you're reasonably accurate in your assessment of your situation. Frequently, during the process of hypothesis testing, one discovers something new and either revises, deletes, or adds to the hypotheses. Drawing conclusions before you've tested your hypotheses risks missing something crucial to the successful resolution of *the* fight in your relationship.

The second reason to test your hypotheses is to more fully and specifically identify *the* fight in your relationship. Remember, you cannot change something until you know what it is. By testing hypotheses, you can play around with them and fine-tune your ideas.

To test your hypotheses, you will need to observe some more interactions with your partner. Again, observe at least 3 or 4 more arguments or every argument that occurs over a 2 to 4-week period. And again, record as much of what happened as you can remember: voice tone, body language, how you felt while you were talking, how you felt while your partner was talking, what was said, and the order in which it was said. Label this "Data Gathering".

There is not much difference between preliminary observations and data gathering. The only difference will be how you use the information. You used your preliminary observations to generate your hypotheses, and you will use your data gathering to confirm or modify them. One reason to observe more interactions is because your preliminary observations and hypotheses generating may have changed how you view these interactions.

Returning to Samantha and Alan for an example, we will observe an argument they had about getting their lawnmower fixed. It was a Sunday morning. Alan had spent some time in his office on Saturday advising another partner's associate about his career. Although this work was not part of his job, he wanted to do it and felt he could not, because of office politics, do it during the workweek. As a result, he hadn't taken the lawn mower to be repaired on Saturday, a job he'd promised to do when he hadn't done it the previous weekend. He could go when the shop opened on Sunday afternoon, but then he'd be late to their son John's basketball game. Both he and Samantha knew from prior experiences that Alan doesn't like to be late to games.

So, she was feeling stuck. If she said nothing, the mower once again wouldn't get fixed, and she'd be angry that she either had to live with an embarrassing lawn or find time to take the mower to the repair shop herself. Either alternative would leave her angry about having to work outside the home and do so much at home while Alan did so little. If she reminded him he'd promised to take the mower last weekend, she anticipated he'd get angry and then she'd get angry and they'd have *the* fight. She felt she had no options that would lead to anything but anger.

Samantha decided she would not take the mower to be repaired, even if the lawn continued to look terrible. She also decided that she wouldn't be angry without saying anything to Alan. So, she decided to remind him to take the mower to be fixed, vowing that she wouldn't allow herself to be drawn into *the* fight about whose job it was to do it. She hoped this approach would reduce her anger and tension, so that she could avoid precipitating *the* fight.

Sitting across the breakfast table from Alan, Samantha began to lose her resolve. She was worried that Alan would be annoyed or sarcastic, and she was uncertain she could disengage from the power struggle over whose job it was to take the mower to be repaired.

The risk for Samantha was that she would become angry about Alan's attitude. The potential benefit, however, would be that, if they could sustain their focus on fixing the lawnmower, she and Alan would not add trash from an argument about fixing the mower to their garbage about *the* fight in their relationship.

> Samantha: Honey, I'd like you to take the mower to the shop on your way to the game today. John and I will meet you there.

Samantha was able to speak calmly and confidently. So, she'd probably reduced the risk of *the* fight by bringing it up without the anger that usually accompanied it.

> Alan [looking up from his paper]: No, I'll go with you.
>
> Samantha [voice tensing]: Then how are you going to get the mower to the shop this weekend?
>
> Alan [sounding reasonable but strained]: I guess it'll have to wait.

Although both Samantha and Alan became tense, their nonverbal communications didn't convey anger at this point. His voice was not raised, and his face had not taken on what Samantha recognized as an angry look. But the strain in his voice might suggest to her that his anger was just beneath the surface. And her tense voice might suggest to him that she was not as calm as she appeared. These reactions confirm my own hypothesis that Samantha and Alan, like any couple, are extremely sensitive to one another's anger about anything related to *the* fight and thus recognize one another's anger no matter how subtly it presents itself.

> Samantha [deep breath]: I'm not sure it can wait.

Alan: Then take it yourself.

Here was the challenge for Samantha. If she declined to take the mower to be repaired, she would risk an argument about whose job it was to do it, and such arguments inevitably led to *the* fight about Samantha working outside the home. On the other hand, if she agreed to take the mower to be fixed, she would be furious at herself for caving in and at Alan for expecting her to do everything.

Samantha [with a tinge of what he referred to as her whining]: You told me you'd do it.

Samantha stuck to the issue of Alan following through on his promises. Her voice tone also contained a challenge, however.

Alan [with sarcasm and condescension]: Well, I ran out of time. I worked yesterday and I have to go to work tomorrow. I'd like to spend this afternoon with my son.

Samantha's whining is associated with Alan's sarcasm and condescension. I'd like to test a hypothesis that the two are related, probably irrespective of whether Samantha whines or Alan becomes sarcastic and condescending first.

Samantha: You could have taken it yesterday, or you could take it today.

Again, Samantha averted the temptation to explain to Alan that he'd only be a few minutes late for the game and would still have most of the afternoon with his son. She also avoided shifting the argument to *the* fight about the relative amounts of time they each worked outside the home and his responsibilities at home.

Alan: Oh, I get it. You're mad that I worked yesterday and you want to punish me. I should have been home doing whatever you wanted me to do here.

Now, his face was tightening with anger as his voice tone became more sarcastic. Was he resisting Samantha's focus, or changing the subject?

Samantha [voice beginning to rise in volume and pitch]: We agreed you'd take the mower in to be fixed this weekend. It's up to you when you do it.

Alan [angry]: Well, I ran out of time. You're the one with all the time on your hands. You do it.

Samantha [angry]: When do you think I'd find the time? I don't have time to do everything you don't feel like doing. I work 30 hours a week and take care of everything for the kids and the house.

Unfortunately, Samantha was distracted by Alan's challenge. She then began defending herself and fell into *the* fight.

Alan [sarcastic]: You'll pardon me if I'm not interested in how hard you work.

Samantha [frustrated, voice rising in volume]: It's not about how hard I work, Alan. It's about *you* not doing things you say you'll do and then expecting *me* to do them as though I don't work at all. I'd really like, just once, to talk about something that needs doing around here without fighting about whether you think I'm working enough.

Although still engaged in *the* fight, Samantha had backed off to the extent that she could address what had happened between them and identify how they had fallen into *the* fight.

Alan [after a pause, voice soft]: Ok.

His voice is quiet, his body relaxing. Samantha, too, no longer looked frustrated and angry.

Alan: I'm going to take a shower.

Not surprisingly, Samantha and Alan were not successful at resolving *the* fight in this situation. However, they were successful in identifying it, and both acknowledged that how much Samantha works outside the home is a fundamental, unresolved issue in their relationship. They also seemed to agree that *the* fight hampers their ability to make even simple, everyday decisions. And finally, acknowledging the presence of *the* fight defused it and prevented the accumulation of more garbage.

Here's how Samantha and Alan described this encounter in their notebooks:

Samantha's Notebook

The Fight with Alan

Data Gathering—Observations

Sunday, 2/24/02—9:30 am:

- I told Alan I wanted him to take the lawn mower to be fixed on his way to John's basketball game. He said, "No."
- We went a couple of rounds about when he would do it without getting angry. I don't remember exactly what we said but he finally said, "Do it yourself."
- I started feeling angry and said, "You said you'd do it."
- He said he didn't have time and then we started fighting about him working all day yesterday and whether I was

mad about that. I don't think I was mad about that; I was mad that he wasn't taking the lawn mower to be fixed like he said he would.

- I said, "You agreed to take it in and the lawn's a mess."
- He said, "I don't have time and you do because you don't work much."
- Then I got really mad and went on about how hard I work. Same old, same old.
- He said he didn't care.
- Somehow, I got it together and told him I was mad because he says he'll do things and then doesn't.

[Note: This was the critical point in the argument. Samantha realized she was angry not only about *the* fight in their relationship but also about Alan not doing things he said he would. And, she brought the argument back from *the* fight to the trash.]

- He said, "OK" and left. And it was ok.

[Note: Translate ok to mean: no new garbage.]

Alan's Notebook

The Fight w/Sam

Data Gathering—Observations

- Samantha was all over me about the lawn mower. She wanted me to take it to the shop on the way to John's game, even though I'd be late.
- I said, "No" and she got upset.
- I thought she was punishing me for working yesterday.
- We started arguing about whether it had to go to the shop today.

- I told her I didn't have time and she could do it during the week and then we started fighting about her working.
- She said she was mad because I don't do what I say I'm going to do and then tell her to do it.

[Note: This is much abbreviated, though very clear that Alan and Samantha both recognized the point of the argument.]

- She might be right. I get mad when she's mad, and I'm tired of hearing about how awful it is that she works. But, I probably need to avoid saying I'll do things and then not do them.

[Note: He also needs to be careful not to react to Samantha's anger by getting angry about how much or how little she works outside the home. I suspect that when Alan is stressed by how much he has to do or defensive in the face of Samantha's anger, he resorts to *the* fight. Samantha, who is more reluctant to express her anger, brings up trash like the lawn mower with the emotional intensity one would expect to accompany *the* fight. Alan probably reacts to her tone, rather than her words and so *the* fight happens anyway.]

At this point, I think it's important to recognize that identifying *the* fight in your relationship, the purpose of this chapter, may increase your pain. Awareness, the first step to change, often brings with it great sadness. As we grasp what's happened to our relationship, we can't avoid realizing how far off track we've strayed. There is hope, however, even in this pain. Identifying *the* fight brings awareness not only of your sadness, but also of your options for resolving *the* fight and changing your relationship into what you want it to be.

Before specifically addressing the how-to of resolving *the* fight and getting your relationship back on track (Chapter 6), I will take you through the steps of analyzing your data and drawing conclusions from your hypothesis testing. Then, we will revisit Samantha and Alan in more detail, as well as the other three couples from Chapter 3, as they identify *the* fight in their relationships (Chapter 5). I recommend you follow the steps in this chapter and read the next before going on to Chapter 6, so that you are as familiar as possible with *the* fight in your own relationship before you attempt to change it. I understand that the pressure to relieve your pain and jump into the how-to of fixing it may be enormous. If you decide to read ahead, I strongly suggest you come back to the end of this chapter and read it and Chapter 5, before you attempt any of the techniques suggested in Chapter 6.

Hypothesis Testing: Analyzing Data

Data analysis is a way of making sense of the information you've got. The observations you recorded in your notebook provide you with information, or data, about *the* fight in your relationship. Your notes also contain details about how *the* fight arises and is perpetuated, and about its consequences. Before you decide whether this information supports or refutes your hypotheses, you need to decide what it means.

In traditional or quantitative research, data can be translated easily into numbers, and those numbers then analyzed statistically. Statistical analyses performed on these numbers are used to identify patterns in the data.

You are also going to look for patterns in your data. Since your data can't be converted to numbers, they will need to be analyzed differently. You are going to use yourself and hopefully your partner, rather than a statistical program and a computer, to look for patterns in what you've observed about your relationship and *the* fight.

Below are seven questions to answer as you analyze your data. These questions are designed to help you think about your observations and identify patterns. The questions invite you to find similarities among the various examples of your observed interactions with your partner. Look for similarities in how *the* fight is triggered, how you feel when it's happening, and how each of you contributes to it. Reread your observations first, and then answer these questions carefully. Record your answers in your notebook in a section called "Data Analysis".

- What does it appear *the* fight in your relationship is about?

At this point, you've observed a number of occurrences of *the* fight. What are the patterns you've seen? In other words, what keeps happening over and over again? You already began to answer this question when you wrote your hypotheses. Based on what you've experienced, seen, and recorded in your notebook since then, you can answer this question more thoroughly now.

Alan and Samantha repeatedly fought about how much (Samantha's view) or how little (Alan's perspective) she works outside the home. Their arguments often referred to differing expectations about and the consequences for who did what at home.

- How do you and your partner get into *the* fight when you begin talking or arguing about something that seems unrelated?

As you reread your observations, notice what happens (verbal and nonverbal communications and your feelings) just before you and your partner shift into *the* fight. Detect the similarities each time this happens. These similarities form the patterns that provide your answer to this question.

For Samantha and Alan, it appears that when one of them becomes frustrated or angry, s/he either provokes (Samantha) or delivers a barb (Alan), and then *the* fight occurs. In the examples in this chapter, they were talking about something Samantha wanted

Alan to do when frustration or anger and a subsequent provocation or barb occurred. Examining their entire notebooks would provide evidence of whether this sequence also occurred when they talked about other things.

- How do you feel just before, during, and after *the* fight?

Before *the* fight happens, Samantha usually feels tense. During *the* fight, she has reported feeling both frustrated and angry. After *the* fight is over, she has felt both sad and angry. She neglected to record in her notebook that after *the* fight on February 2nd she felt hopeless; when Alan left the table, she sat and cried. She had a different experience on February 24th, when *the* fight ended in a unique way and she said she felt ok.

Alan was extremely forthright in his notebook about his own anger in response to Samantha's. Apparently, he picks up on her tension before *the* fight happens and begins to express anger then. Samantha usually responds by becoming angry herself, if she isn't already, or more angry if she is. It's unclear what Alan feels after *the* fight is over. At this point in the analysis, it would be helpful for him to observe another example of *the* fight with attention to his feelings after it is finished.

As you can see, tracking both your own and your partner's feelings provides insight into how *the* fight plays out. The sequence of Samantha becoming tense, Alan getting angry, and then Samantha becoming angry herself is very important. Lucy, Samantha's therapist, thought she avoided anger, but Lucy never saw her provoke Alan. This sequence demonstrates how Samantha's anger avoidance operates in the relationship and thus points the way to change (Chapter 6).

- What are your thoughts about how your partner feels just before, during, and after *the* fight?

You can't observe how your partner feels, but you probably have some thoughts about how s/he feels. Even though these thoughts aren't observations, they influence your behavior and thus are important, so include them here. If you are working with your partner on these exercises, s/he will be able to tell you how s/he feels. It might be interesting to each write down what you assume the other feels and then compare notes to see how accurate you were.

Samantha tended to view Alan as angry, while he more often viewed her as whiny and demanding. Alan and Samantha both saw themselves as provoked to anger, rather than its instigator.

- What do you and your partner do that intensifies *the* fight?

Examine your notebook and think about what has happened during *the* fight that has intensified it. Because you will have many examples, notice whether what you have identified occurs in most iterations of *the* fight.

Alan's sarcastic remarks intensified *the* fight. And, Samantha's sense that she was losing focus while Alan labeled her behavior as whiny often occurred at about the time the argument became *the* fight. So, they might conclude that her whininess and his sarcasm intensified the argument, if not *the* fight itself.

- Have you noticed anything either of you does that may diminish the intensity of *the* fight?

Again, examine your notebook and think about what has happened during *the* fight that has changed its intensity. This time, however, notice what has diminished its force. When Samantha "somehow got it together" on the 24th and told Alan what was really bothering her, the intensity of their fight diminished and they ended it feeling better about each other. If she were able to repeat the process, they could conclude that Samantha stating her feelings diminished the intensity of *the* fight.

- Is there anything else you observed while testing your hypotheses?

This is the place to mention anything you haven't already included in an answer to one of the other six questions. If you've observed another a pattern, or dynamic, it's important to put it in your notebook. The more you know, the more options you will have to resolve *the* fight and change its negative influence on your relationship.

Throughout this chapter, I've added my comments and analyses of Samantha and Alan's fights. These comments also serve as examples of analyses.

Here are Samantha and Alan's entries about data analysis from their notebooks. I've added comments about their entries, rather than analyses of the arguments.

Samantha's notebook

The Fight with Alan

Data Analysis

- I think *the* fight in our relationship is about Alan wanting me to work full time and me wanting to be at home with the kids. I also think we have a second important fight about which of us decides what Alan will do around here.
- We get into *the* fight whenever I ask Alan to do something. He seems to think he doesn't have to do anything he doesn't want to because I'm not working full time, so then we start fighting about me working instead of whatever I've asked him to do. And I'm often angry about his

attitude, which reminds me how angry I am about working. Another way we get into *the* fight is when I've tried to keep us on target and Alan won't cooperate—like he has the power to decide what I can ask him to do *and* what we can talk about. I think I need another hypothesis about power. It's an important issue in our marriage.

[Note: Samantha could either write her thoughts about the new hypothesis here, or amend her hypotheses in the "Conclusions" section of her notebook. She included them here so that you could follow her thought processes, although I recommend you keep your hypotheses together.]

- Before *the* fight I want to have a conversation with my husband and have us work as a team. During *the* fight, I feel angry about his attitude and about working and hurt that he doesn't seem to care about me. After *the* fight, when I'm not angry anymore, I often feel sad.
- Alan looks like he's tense and wary the minute I start talking to him. I guess he feels like I'm going to demand something from him or attack him or something. He seems to want to stop me from talking about whatever I want to talk about.

[Note: Samantha was not examining the nonverbal message she communicated to Alan. It may be that he heard the demand, as she suspected. It may also be that he heard the tension and knew she was angry. In other words, he may have reacted to Samantha's hidden anger by trying to stop her from talking about whatever had angered her.]

- *The* fight intensifies when I don't back off when he asks and when he gets sarcastic or talks to me like I'm an idiot. I guess he gets angrier when I don't back off, and I get angry when he gets sarcastic with me. And I get angry when he doesn't want to talk.

- The intensity of *the* fight went down when I told him I wanted to talk about something that needed doing around the house without fighting about me working.
- I observed how hopeless I feel about our ability to resolve our fight. I also noticed that even when Alan directly addresses his feelings about my work, I don't tell him how angry and sad I am about it. I noticed that Alan still initiates *the* fight, even though I'm bolder about conflict and am also angry. It's puzzling that I'm furious about working but we only seem to fight about it when he brings it up.

Alan's notebook

The Fight with Sam

Data Analysis

- *The* fight is about how Sam changed after the kids were born and she stopped wanting to work.
- Samantha tries to hide her anger, but I can tell. She gets whiny. She usually wants me to do something and I think, she's home a lot during the week, let her do it.
- I'm tired of Sam picking fights with me and then saying she's not mad.
- Samantha's always tense when she starts one of these conversations.

[Note: Although he wrote in an abbreviated manner, Alan had picked up on several important aspects of his fight with Samantha. His input from this observation will be critical to identifying *the* fight, as we shall see. For the moment, it's important to remember that Samantha cried *after* he left the room on February 2nd. Alan was not disregarding her sadness; he didn't see it.]

- We get angry and then we can't fix whatever we're fighting about. She won't even admit that she's angry. And when I'm angry, I get sarcastic, which Sam doesn't like.
- We get less angry when we talk about what's really bothering us, without being sarcastic or pretending we're not angry.

[Note: It strikes me that Alan must be very angry about Samantha's efforts to control, or hide, her frustration and anger. This entry seems to account for his sarcasm when it apparently erupts from nowhere during their arguments.]

- I'm angry at Sam's unilateral decision not to resume her career. And then when she wants to talk or tells me to do something around here, that anger gets involved.

[Note that Samantha continued to work ¾-time outside the home. While they appear to agree that her career has a different trajectory now, the number of hours she works does not appear to have been a unilateral decision on Alan's part. It would be interesting to know how they negotiated her career change and what issues that now appear in *the* fight were present or even originated then.]

These seven questions are designed to reveal the patterns in your data. The answers, in addition to the observations you've recorded, may expose those elements that repeatedly precipitate and intensify *the* fight in your relationship. Your answers may also provide clues about how to reduce *the* fight's intensity.

As you've read the excerpts from Samantha and Alan's notebooks, you may have noticed that neither is completely accurate about what was going on between them. Yet, when we combined their notebooks, a more consistent picture emerged. This is one of the reasons I recommend you work with your partner to identify *the* fight in your relationship. However, as noted earlier in this chapter, working alone may also be helpful.

It's quite clear that *the* fight in Samantha and Alan's relationship occurs when she wants him to do something. She may already be angry that he hasn't done it. Or, she may be tense about asking. After all, she avoids conflict, and asking seems to precipitate conflict in their relationship. I suspect it's a chicken-and-egg phenomenon, but Samantha has focused on the asking-leads-to-Alan's-anger part of the cycle, whereas Alan has focused on the Samantha's-anger-leads-to-Alan's-anger phenomenon.

Clearly, Alan recognizes and reacts to her tension and/or anger. He becomes angry himself, both about her anger and about how much she's changed her attitude about her career. At this point, his anger is associated with his belief that since she's home more than he is, she should do more than she does. She, on the other hand, believes that Alan fails to account for the number of hours she still works outside the home.

Thus, Samantha's requests, whether for a chores schedule or a lawn mower repair, get deflected into *the* fight, and issues of power, caring, and the responsibilities of a good partner, arise. As they become sidetracked, Samantha and Alan lose sight of whatever Samantha was asking for in the first place. At the end of *the* fight, they walk away frustrated, angry, and sometimes sad, with no resolution about who is going to do whatever Samantha wants done or of *the* fight about her career. At this point, one or the other or both is angry about Samantha's changed attitude about work, how Alan has responded to it, how they haven't dealt with their respective feelings about each other's attitudes, and how they haven't dealt with the impact of the change on what they expect from one another at home. Identifying *the* fight may lead them to remain focused on their anger and the issues with which they haven't yet dealt, thus providing them options for resolving *the* fight and reducing its negative consequences for their relationship (Chapter 6).

Drawing Conclusions

Once you've analyzed your data, you can then determine whether it supports or refutes your hypotheses. You can also decide whether you left a question out of your original hypotheses and add it. If you find yourself adding a question, it might be helpful to answer it as part of identifying *the* fight in your relationship. A real scientist would need to collect new data to answer a research question that arose during the analysis. For our purposes, it would be alright to review your notebook and decide whether anything you've recorded helps you answer the new question. If not, then consider observing more arguments with your partner.

Prior to generating conclusions, first reread the "Hypotheses", "Observations", and "Data Analysis" sections of your notebook. Then, answer the four questions listed below. Write the answers to these questions in your notebook in a section called "Conclusions".

- Did your data gathering and analysis confirm any of your hypotheses or answer any of the research questions posed in your hypotheses? Which one(s)?
- Did your data gathering and analysis lead you to reject any of your hypotheses? Which one(s)?
- Did your observations lead you to rethink any of your original hypotheses or questions? How would you rewrite your original hypotheses or questions?
- Did your observations lead you to any new hypotheses or questions about your relationship?

Before you read the "Conclusions" sections of Samantha and Alan's notebooks, I want to remind you that they cannot possibly draw conclusions from the one argument I've included from their notebooks in the hypothesis testing section of this chapter. One example simply can't provide enough information to answer these questions. You'll need to observe at least three or four arguments to draw your conclusions, as I've recommended. Samantha and Alan used four, even though I've only included dialogue from one of them.

Samantha's notebook

The Fight with Alan

Conclusions

- My observations confirmed my first hypothesis.
- I'm not sure being reminded gets Alan angry, so I'm not sure my second hypothesis is right.

[Note: Samantha couldn't possibly observe Alan being reminded. On the other hand, her second hypothesis was too general to test. She was accurate, however, that something between them angered Alan; it's how indirectly she expresses her anger.]

- I'd rewrite the second hypothesis to say *the* fight happens when we're fighting about which of us is responsible for what.
- I now have another hypothesis: When Alan turns a conversation or argument to the topic of him wanting me to work more, I feel defensive and we have *the* fight.

Alan's notebook

The Fight with Samantha

Conclusions

- 1st hypothesis confirmed; 2nd hypothesis somewhat true.
- Neither rejected.

- Sam gets mad when she wants me to do something.
- It might help if Samantha told me when she's angry about asking me to do something.

[Note: Samantha anticipated that Alan would resist her request and got tense before the conversation even began. Alan interpreted this tension as anger, and so the pattern of their interactions that leads to *the* fight began, thus confirming Samantha's expectation.]

Alan and Samantha's awareness of the dynamics of *the* fight in their relationship increased when they compared their notebooks. While their original hypotheses reflected their anger at one another, their conclusions revealed their ability to modulate that anger and view their relationship more clearly.

Alan and Samantha's notebooks don't reflect the greater awareness each now has of her/his contribution to *the* fight, because they didn't change what they'd already written after they compared their notebooks. However, their increased recognition of their own contributions to *the* fight remained an important step toward resolving it.

Summary

Before you complete the exercises in this chapter, I recommend that you read Chapter 5 for more examples. When you've finished, then do the exercises in this chapter.

When you've finished the exercises, you will have taken a huge step toward identifying *the* fight in your relationship. You will have observed, identified patterns, hypothesized about how these patterns replay in your arguments and how you and your partner respond, tested your hypotheses, revised your hypotheses, and drawn conclusions.

Your awareness of what *the* fight is about, you and your partner's reactions to it, and the impact of your partner's reaction on you will have increased. If you've done the exercises together, you've also learned something about how your reaction affects your partner. If you've done them alone, you have at least thought about how you might affect your partner. As you read Chapter 5, record any thoughts you have about your relationship in your notebook, under the heading "Additional Thoughts." You can also use this section of your notebook to record what you've learned from your partner's notebook if you've worked separately and then compared notebooks, as Alan and Samantha did.

Before you continue, take a moment to consider how much thought, time, and energy you've already put into the project of identifying *the* fight in your relationship. That tremendous effort bodes well for your future. So, stop here, and congratulate yourself. You might even consider rewarding yourself. Do something you really enjoy. If you've been working with your partner, think of something you used to love to do together, but haven't done recently, and do it now.

5

More Stories about Couples and Their Fights

In Chapter 3 you met four couples whose stories exemplify the nine issues that frequently underlie *the* fight in a relationship. Now I will tell you about how these four couples went about identifying *the* fight in their relationships.

Alan and Samantha worked separately on their notebooks, as you saw in Chapter 3. Adele and John worked separately on their previous research and feelings and then came together to generate and analyze data to test hypotheses and draw conclusions. Pete declined to participate, so Shelly worked alone. Serena and Brad began separate notebooks, but soon devolved into *the* fight and then went on to Chapter 6 without completing the identification process.

Alan and Samantha: Working Separately

Alan and Samantha did an excellent job of identifying *the* fight and then avoided being drawn into arguments about trash as they compared their notebooks (Chapter 4). You've read enough of their notebooks that I'll exclude further examples here.

In Chapter 3, they alluded to an older fight about spending time together. Although they no longer disagreed about spending time together, it's important they remain alert for this fight recurring in the future. Couples become particularly vulnerable to re-emerging fights after they've resolved *the* fight in their relationship, as well as immediately after children are born and when they leave home.

The garbage in Alan and Samantha's relationship was a product of the history of each one's anger at the other. When Samantha believed her problem was Alan's insensitivity and rage and when Alan believed his problem stemmed from Samantha being unreasonable and uncooperative, they expressed frustration by attacking one another's behavior and attitudes. Garbage arose from the feelings being attacked generated in each.

Working separately on their notebooks allowed Alan and Samantha to become clearer about their own contributions to *the* fight and the patterns that had developed between them. Working together might have diverted them back into the fight.

Adele and John: Working Together

Adele and John initially kept separate notebooks.

_____

Adele's Notebook

Previous Research

- My therapist said I allow my mother and sisters to make me feel guilty.
- My therapist said I allow my mother to manipulate me into spending time with her.
- My therapist said I want to think things will be different with my mother and sisters, but they never are.
- I want John to continue supporting my efforts to keep distance, but I also want him to go along with me when I want to see them or think I should. I think—I'm confused.
- Reading about loyalty and boundaries in Chapter 2 made me think a lot of my problems with my family are about them [the issues of boundaries and loyalty]. I also wonder whether John cares about me as much as

he used to. [Notice Adele apparently did not recognize intimacy, and more specifically John taking care of her emotionally, as a theme in her marriage.]

- My friends think family is very important and don't understand my dread of moving closer, even when I tell them how awful my mother and sisters can be.
- Is this entirely my problem? Or, does John have a responsibility to honor my wishes?

Feelings

- Confusion about what I ask of John—where we live and family time.
- Sadness and anger that my mother and sisters manipulate me, I let myself feel guilty, they don't like me, or want me to be me, and they're not going to change—I really don't want to feel this.
- Anger and sadness that John isn't protecting me like he used to, maybe doesn't even respect or care about me like he used to—what have I done? Or not done?

John's Notebook

Previous Research

- In our session with Adele's therapist, she pointed out we really hadn't discussed what I want after the kids leave home.
- I haven't communicated well about how much I want to slow down, but I only just started thinking about it.
- Adele hasn't treated my needs about family time as important over the years and now she's not treating my need to slow down as important, either [theme of respect and importance].
- I can't fix Adele's family for her.

Feelings

- I'm angry about all the times I've caved in and we've spent holidays and vacations with her family. Now the kids have their own lives, and we don't have family vacations to look back on.
- I guess I'm also angry about how Adele's ignored what I wanted for our family and now my wish to work with Mike.
- I want to slow down badly. Mike's life sounds great. I want Adele to understand how important this is to me.

I suspect John was also sad that he couldn't make life happier for his mother after her divorce or Adele's relationships with her mother and sisters easier for her. His role as caretaker to his mother explained the ease with which he fell into protecting Adele from her family and hiding his upset about their impact.

Adele and John captured the essence, not only of their relationship, but also of their sense of themselves, in these notebook entries. I am especially struck by John's self-demeaning attitude ("I haven't communicated well..."). It wasn't until he began to link his and Adele's relationship dynamics to the issues of respect and importance that he moved outside his self-criticism and into his upset with her behavior.

Similarly, Adele appeared fairly self-centered. Although she questioned her role, she continued to shovel responsibility to John.

Given this dynamic in their relationship, Adele and John got along amazingly well. When *the* fight is about one partner wishing to relinquish either caretaking or being taken care of, couples frequently cannot work together at all. The caretaker sometimes becomes fed up with the responsibility, while the one taken care of resists relinquishing being indulged. Alternatively, the one who has been taken care of may be angry about being treated like a child, while the caretaker resists giving up the caretaking role.

Up to this point, their relationship roles (John-as-caretaker, Adele-as-who-it's-all-about) have complemented their roles as breadwinner and homemaker. But Adele wished to move beyond her role as homemaker, while John wanted to change his work life. This shift may have shaken what had been a stable situation. And it's important to remember that John and Adele's wishes to change their roles happened irrespective of the impact on Adele's relationship with her mother and sisters.

For many couples, a shift toward more equitable roles out in the world requires a parallel change within the relationship. That Adele and John shared the goal of transitioning work roles may lessen their difficulties around transforming their relationship roles.

Unlike Alan and Samantha, *the* fight in Adele and John's relationship did not arise out of the daily fabric of their lives. They were able to generate and observe *the* fight in their relationship only by talking about their plans for their son's high school graduation and how their lives would change at the end of the summer, when he left home. So, they decided to talk about the decisions associated with these events, with the specific goal of precipitating *the* fight.

They brought their notebooks, hiked at a nearby state park, and talked about their plans while eating a picnic lunch. At this point, they began keeping a single notebook.

John: Ok, Adele. I've been thinking that perhaps you're right; I shouldn't ask you to move.

Adele: [smiling] That would be great.

John [no accompanying smile]: Yeah, it would. The problem is, I wouldn't be happy. I'd just be doing what you want me to do. And, I'm not sure I can just do that anymore.

Adele [placating]: Honey, you talked about wanting to slow down. Isn't there a way to slow down here?

John: Not that we can afford.

Adele [a touch of panic creeping into her voice]: What if I got a job? I don't have to go back to school, or open a teashop. I could work, and then you could afford to slow down and we could stay here.

John [angry]: Yeah, we could. But that isn't the point. Damn it, Adele. The point is that your mother and sisters have been controlling our lives ever since I can remember. And soon the kids will all have their own lives, and we don't even have family vacations to remember.

Adele: I don't see what family vacations have to do with the plans we make now.

John: It's just another example of me accommodating to your inability to deal with your mother and sisters. And I'm sick of it, Adele. I've been doing it for years, not thinking about what I've given up. And now I'm thinking about it and I can't keep doing it anymore.

Adele [quietly]: I don't think that's fair, John.

At this point, another group of hikers arrived to picnic within hearing distance, so Adele and John agreed to stop the conversation and record what had happened.

I suspect Adele and John had avoided *the* fight for quite awhile. John's reluctance to ask Adele to confront her mother was palpable; after all, he had taken the role of soothing the pain of important women in his life, not augmenting it by insisting his own needs be prioritized. So until he discovered that his desire to change his work situation converged on a need to move closer to Adele's family, he lacked the motivation to press his point. But once he recognized his need for Adele to resolve her issues with her mother and sisters, his anger at both himself and Adele about the consequences of not challenging her sooner surfaced.

When Adele resisted his decision to move, John's anger about what they'd given up as a family in order to accommodate her parents rose to the surface. John knew he couldn't reclaim the family vacations they'd forfeited to Adele's parents, and this realization only aggravated his distress about their son Jeff leaving home.

At the same time, Adele assumed John was happy to go along with her requests to spend time with her parents. Because he never expressed divergent wishes, she remained unaware of his true feelings. She therefore assumed his anger meant he didn't care about her as much as he had previously. She became hurt and then angry. However, Adele's anger was about John changing, whereas John's anger focused on his own and Adele's earlier behavior.

The fight in John and Adele's relationship was about how they as a couple relate to Adele's family of origin. John's anger at himself and at Adele about the past was garbage that exacerbated *the* fight about where they would live now and in the future. Additionally, Adele's anger at John's desire to change the relationship contract regarding her family of origin and hurt that he seemed to care less about her aggravated the situation by adding other issues to *the* fight.

John had initiated their discussion by talking about his disinclination to ask Adele to move. The transition from the question of moving to John's anger happened almost immediately. When Adele responded with enthusiasm to the idea that John would pass up the opportunity to work with Mike so that she would not have to live closer to her parents and sisters, John got angry not only about the sacrifices she was asking him to make now but also about those he had made over the course of their childrearing years. As so often happens, a strong emotion in the present reminds us of similar emotions from or about the past.

In the previous conversation, Adele and John got right to the point. In the following example, they discussed their youngest child's high school graduation, and the transition to *the* fight in their relationship was more subtle.

Adele: Are your mother and Bob coming to graduation?

John: I haven't spoken to them yet about it—it's four months away—but I think, yes. Why?

Adele: Well, I know my parents are coming, and I'm trying to figure out whether I need to make hotel reservations for anyone.

John: Didn't we decide some time ago that if your parents ever visited it'd be better if they stayed in a hotel? You've talked about how miserable it would be to have your mother following you around the house criticizing you.

I find it stunning that although Adele has lived for over 30 years in a community within a day's drive and an hour's flight from where her parents live, they've never visited her.

Adele: Yes, but they'd be so hurt.

John: Then we can put Mom and Bob in a hotel, too, and you can tell your parents no one is staying with us.

Adele: Jennie and Jill [their older children] are coming home for Jeff's graduation. And Jill will probably bring Rich.

John: It'll be pretty crowded here. You have a good excuse.

Adele: Well, go ahead and tell your mom and Bob we'll get them a hotel room, and I'll see what happens with my parents.

John [hesitating]: You know, it might be a good idea to try telling your parents something they don't want to hear.

Adele [suspiciously]: Why? Oh, no. So, I can start practicing for the move? Is that what you're saying?

John: Adele, Honey.

Adele: Don't "Honey" me. You used to *care* about how my mother makes me feel. You used to *want* to help me deal with her. Or maybe you were just pretending?

When John hesitated before suggesting that Adele broach this difficult subject with her parents, he might have thought, this isn't fair. He also may have seen an opportunity to make a point. Whatever went through his mind, his statement shifted the discussion from the logistics of graduation to *the* fight.

Adele and John wrote a description of these two arguments in their combined notebook. They agreed on four observations and two hypotheses.

Adele and John's combined notebook

Observations:

- We won't know where we're going to live and what we can afford to do until we resolve *the* fight about Adele's family;
- Now that we've questioned how Adele's family affects us, we can't talk about our future or anything involving Adele's parents without risking *the* fight;

- Adele wants John to go back to the way he was [about her family] and gets angry when he persists [in changing]; she also knows she hasn't been happy about how things go with her parents and has felt guilty and angry at them when she and John have done things to make them [her parents and sisters] happy that haven't made them [John and Adele] happy;
- John stops himself sometimes [from saying what he means] because he doesn't want to hurt Adele; lately, he's too angry to [stop himself].

Hypotheses:

- *The* fight is about the impact of Adele's family on our lives, including how we've spent holidays and vacations and now our choice about what to do when Jeff goes to college;
- We've both been angry and felt guilty about how we've handled Adele's family for much longer than we've admitted [note: it's impossible to test "much longer"; "our anger and guilt about how we've handled Adele's family surfaces when we talk about anything related to them" might be a hypothesis about behavior that is easier to observe].

Adele and John then kept notes about more incidents of *the* fight and got together to analyze their data. This took them about a month.

In Chapter 4, I listed seven questions to help you analyze your data about *the* fight in your relationship. Adele and John answered the questions together. I'm going to include their discussion, rather than their notebook, to illustrate the process.

John: Ok, the first question is, and "What does it appear *the* fight in your relationship is about?" I think we've got that.

Adele: Yeah.

Apparently, Adele and John didn't observe anything that contradicted their first hypothesis. Of course, a real scientist would argue that what they saw was biased by what they expected to see. Even so, I think it's safe to agree that *the* fight in their relationship is about the impact of Adele's family on their lives.

John: "How do you and your partner get into *the* fight...?" What do you think?

Adele: When we try to plan, you know, like about graduation or next fall.

John: Yeah. And I noticed we also get into it more lately when either of us is upset. I found myself wanting to yell at you one night last week when I'd had a rough day and I wanted you to see how tired I was and say, "Of course we'll move so you can work with Mike." I was kind of fried that you didn't say that.

Adele: Put that in there: that *the* fight is about me not reading your mind. My therapist would love that.

John [laughing]: Ok. Point taken.

Adele [giggles]: Thank you.

John: Ok, next: "How do you feel just before, during, and after *the* fight?" Is it my turn?

Adele: Umhm.

John: Angry. That's too obvious, though.

Adele: Yep. What else?

John: I want to turn the clock back. When we start talking about the future, I want to turn the clock back and do things differently in the past. I think what's really happening is that I'm sad about Jeff leaving. The kids are great, and we know from Jenny and Jilly that things change when they go to college. I know it's time, but I want my kids back.

Adele [tearful]: I know. Me, too. That's why I get excited about doing something new. But, you know, the something new I want to do isn't going back and fixing my relationship with my mother and sisters.

John: Yeah, but you've got to.

Adele: I'm not convinced.

John: Adele, I need you to.

They've moved away from analyzing data and back into *the* fight. And this presents a difficult situation for them: they need to somehow talk about *the* fight without having it. In Chapter 6, I'll describe a tool for accomplishing this very difficult task, called metacommunication. For the time being, we'll let them finish *the* fight and rejoin them as they move on to answer the question about how they feel.

Adele: Ok, now we know how angry we are before *the* fight. Are you up for answering the part about during and after?

John: Well, we just went though it. Let's see, angry during and not so great after.

Adele: Yeah, I feel better this time, but usually I feel like I don't even want to know you afterward. And that makes me sad. I really don't like how you've changed. You used to understand so well how my mother and sisters make me feel. Did you stop caring about me, or what?

John: No. I suddenly realized how much I'd given up by being understanding, and I just don't think I can do it [give those things up?] anymore.

Adele and John once again are off on a tangent and may resume *the* fight, as well. Working together at this point risks recurrences of *the* fight. If you decide to work together before finishing your notebook entries, expect to spend at least two or three sessions analyzing data, because you'll probably want to take a break every time you repeat or notice yourselves starting to repeat *the* fight.

John: Ok, "What are your thoughts about how your partner feels...?" I think we've answered that for each other. So, "What do you and your partner do that intensifies *the* fight?" When you say you don't want to change how you deal with your mother, I get even angrier. What about you?

Adele: I don't know. I guess when you push me to change I get angrier.

John: Ok. "Have you noticed anything either of you does that may diminish the intensity of *the* fight?"

Adele: When you back off. But I think it's when you feel guilty.

John is a rescuer. His guilt happens when he thinks he "should" be rescuing Adele from the discomfort she feels about being near or changing her relationships with her mother and sisters.

John: Well, I feel less angry when you acknowledge that there is a problem between you and your mother. When you've let me know it bothers you, I feel like at least we're on the same page.

Adele: Ok, next question?

John: Last question: "Is there anything else you observed while testing your hypotheses?"

Adele: I don't think so.

John: Well, that we can talk about this, at least. That makes me feel better.

Adele: You're right. It'd be a lot harder if we just fought about it and couldn't talk. It makes us closer, and I guess that makes *the* fight less intense.

The final step of the four-step method for identifying *the* fight in your relationship is drawing conclusions (Chapter 4). Adele and John completed this task together, as well. Their dialogue was very similar to the conversation about data analysis. Let's turn now to the third couple, Pete and Shelly.

Pete and Shelly: Working Alone

Shelly hoped that working together to identify and change *the* fight would help her feel closer to Pete again. So, she asked him whether he'd be willing to work on a series of exercises to help improve their communication. He declined, claiming he thought they were getting along fine except for Shelly's affair and her un-substantiated worry about him. And she experienced his refusal to participate as another example of him pulling away from her, and felt sadder and more hopeless about their relationship.

Shelly assured Pete that her affair was brief and finished. Pete contended that he had to work out his feelings about it on his own. Although he offered to reconsider working together to iden-tify and resolve *the* fight at a later time, Shelly felt uncertain about their future and therefore a sense of urgency to proceed before she gave up on their relationship. As a result, she decided to do the exercises on her own.

Shelly found herself experiencing wildly fluctuating feelings about Pete. Some days, she wanted to be with him and felt affectionate toward him. At other times, she found herself furious and wanting to be with someone who understood and talked to her, like Andrew.

So, with a mixture of reluctance and hope, she undertook the process of identifying *the* fight in their relationship on her own. Her initial attempts resulted in a lot of information about Pete and not much about herself.

Shelly's notebook

Previous Research & Feelings

- Pete has become quiet, withdrawn, and lost interest [she doesn't know this; all she can observe is his refusal to participate] in our social life.
- Pete is becoming more and more like his father [how?].
- Pete is denying his anger about my affair [at least to me].
- Pete won't do this exercise with me; even though I told him I'm worried our relationship is falling apart, he continued to refuse.
- Whenever I try to get close to Pete, I feel like a shrew, like a sober version of his mother.
- I'm angry with Pete for denying his depression and anger about my affair.

Shelly focused almost entirely on Pete, his depression, and his passivity, rather than on the relationship and herself. Alan and Samantha demonstrated by working separately on their notebooks that a couple doesn't have to work together to identify *the* fight. However, for Shelly, Pete's refusal to participate epitomized her anger, placing it front and center in her life.

To identify *the* fight, Shelly must shift her focus from what's wrong with Pete to what she knows about herself and about her relationship with him. When she listed and went on to test her hypotheses, she realized they were about her dissatisfaction with Pete and not about the relationship. To identify *the* fight in their relationship, she returned to her notebook and rewrote her entries.

Shelly's notebook

Previous Research & Feelings

- Pete has always spent more time alone when he's stressed. He's always said no to social events when he's stressed.
- I've always felt scared when Pete's withdrawn from our friends and me. [I wonder what her fear is about.]
- I'm angry with Pete for not hearing how unhappy and lonely I've been and for not defending [how?] our relationship.
- I am angry at myself for getting involved with Andrew.
- I am angry with Pete for how quiet he is; even when he's not stressed, he never wants to talk about our future or us—he even said it was up to me whether we have a child.
- I have wanted this relationship to work and have done everything I could think of. I feel Pete hasn't [how does she observe this?]. Now, I feel like giving up.
- I don't have a clue what Pete is feeling. He says everything is fine and I just have to give him space. I don't believe him that everything is fine, and I need to feel closer to him, rather than more distant. [Would giving him more space lead her to feel more distant?]
- Whenever I try to get close to Pete, I feel like a shrew, like a sober version of his mother.

- The issue I think best fits us is intimacy. We don't have any kind of intimacy—physical or emotional. I guess I miss both, or I wouldn't have gotten involved with Andrew.
- Distance regulation is also an issue in our relationship: I want more closeness; he wants more distance.
- My friends say I compare myself to everyone else and always think I'm not as good. I haven't asked if they think I do this with Pete, too.

Shelly's fear when Pete withdrew was a fascinating revelation. In recognizing this reaction to Pete, she acknowledged at least part of her role in their relationship. In other words, her fear was probably associated with certain behaviors, both verbal and nonverbal, and Pete likely reacted to these behaviors in a consistent manner when they appeared. While Shelly needed to be more specific about her behaviors and Pete's reactions, her observation was a start to learning to observe *the* fight with Pete.

Identifying this dynamic will allow Shelly to be more specific and then to initiate changes in her relationship with Pete. Until this point, she had recognized only two solutions to their problems: Pete could change his behavior and possibly his personality; or she could end their relationship. She had no control over Pete's changes and didn't want to divorce him. So, she felt stuck. Now there's also the possibility that she can soothe herself when she is afraid, rather than initiating the cycle of fear and response with Pete. Shelly's dilemma exemplified how identification can release you from all-or-nothing dichotomies and redirect you toward other options (Chapter 6).

After revising her notebook entry, Shelly moved on to generate hypotheses.

_____

Shelly's notebook

Hypotheses

- When Pete withdraws, I get scared and try to pull him closer. Then, *the* fight is about how much space he can have.
- When we have *the* fight, I think we are like his parents and I get angry with both of us.
- When I gave up that Pete and I could be close, I got involved with Andrew; I need to do something besides fighting with Pete about closeness or leaving him for someone else when I'm upset with Pete's distance.

Her third hypothesis isn't really a testable hypothesis, but Shelly is absolutely correct in concluding that she needs more options.

As with the other two couples, increasing awareness of the relationship dynamics embedded in *the* fight helped Shelly feel better disposed toward Pete. So, she again asked him to help her identify *the* fight. He again declined. Rather than showing him her anger and disappointment, Shelly viewed his rebuff of her overture as an example of distance regulation and, while she didn't like it, she was able to view his behavior with empathy and avoid reacting in the manner that led to *the* fight, at least for the moment. By reacting differently, she avoided another repetition of *the* fight and ensuing garbage.

Despite this success in avoiding *the* fight when Pete declined to participate in identifying it, Shelly had many opportunities to observe *the* fight over the next few weeks and diligently wrote about it in her notebook.

Shelly: Pete, I think we need to decide about a baby.

Pete: Are you kidding? I need some time.

Shelly: Well, can we talk about it?

Pete: Not now.

At this point, Shelly assumed she had two options: she could either push forward and risk *the* fight or drop the subject and feel angry and hopeless about being with Pete.

Here's a second example of how *the* fight developed, this time from less emotionally loaded content.

Shelly: Sue and Judy are coming into town next weekend.

Pete: And?

Shelly: I'd like to invite them to stay here, so we can spend more time with them.

Pete: You go ahead.

Shelly: I'd like *us* to spend time with them, not just me.

Pete: I don't know what I'll be doing next weekend.

Shelly [sarcastically]: What do you ever do?

Pete: Look, Shelly, they're your friends. I'm not stopping you from seeing them, or even inviting them to stay here. Just don't ask me to make plans this far ahead.

And, finally, here's an excerpt from an argument about Shelly's relationship with Andrew.

Shelly: I've got to go to Atlanta next week for a couple of days. I tried to get out of it, but Pam [her boss] said I couldn't miss this one.

Pete: Fine.

Shelly: Really? I thought you didn't want me to travel anymore.

Pete: It's your decision.

Shelly: Yeah, but….

Pete [condescendingly]: If you're willing to take the risk, there's not much I can do about it.

Shelly: And you're not even upset?

Pete [angry]: Look, Shelly, I clearly can't stop you from doing whatever you want. And I'm not about to become some macho guy who tries to run your life for you.

Shelly: Yeah, but….

Pete [turning away]: That's it. You decide for yourself what to do.

Next, Shelly analyzed her data and drew conclusions. Her data confirmed the hypothesis that *the* fight is about distance and closeness. Shelly observed that most of the time, when she and Pete talked about doing something together, she worked to draw them closer together while he worked to create more distance between them. She realized that she usually initiated the conversations that led to *the* fight, and that she felt lonely and scared before she did. As their conversations turned into *the* fight, first hurt and then anger replaced her loneliness and fear. Backing off diminished the intensity of *the* fight, but left it unresolved.

Shelly speculated that Pete experienced her attempts at closeness as demands on his time and energy. She suspected that during *the* fight he felt attacked. She even wondered whether she was communicating that he'd failed her. Perhaps, she thought, he's concluded that's why I got involved with Andrew. After *the* fight, Pete seemed to Shelly to be relieved it was over and he had an excuse to be angry and refuse to talk to her.

She concluded that her desire for closeness was unreciprocated by Pete and that her way of changing their relationship (initiating more closeness) wasn't effective. Although she successfully identified *the* fight in their relationship, she felt even more hopeless than when she began. Although her anguish might have been increased by Pete's refusal to participate in identifying *the* fight, the reason Pete declined is the reason Shelly was unhappy: his apparent need for more distance. So, she felt worse after identifying *the* fight because she became hopeless about her options for resolving it.

One problem with Shelly's analysis is that it neglects her need for distance and Pete's need for closeness. As long as she is agitating for more closeness and Pete is resisting, she needn't worry about feeling too close or he about drifting too far apart. As long as she remained focused on how scared, sad, and angry she felt when he pulled away; she never saw what she would feel if he didn't. Had they worked together, they might have found that their roles served a purpose in their relationship, as well as leading to *the* fight.

Shelly's predicament illustrates how identifying *the* fight can lead to feeling worse, rather than better. Even though I can see her third option, she could not. If you share her experience, you, like Shelly, need to continue your quest. I can't emphasize enough that options always exist. Continuing on to Chapter 6 will help Shelly find hers, as you will see in Chapter 7.

Serena and Brad: Blocked

Serena approached Brad about working together on the exercises in Chapter 4. He agreed, but suggested they decide whether they wanted to stay together before working on their relationship.

Serena proposed that working on the relationship might help them make the decision about continuing it. They were in a chicken-and-egg dilemma. Serena's willingness to devote more time by working first and then deciding may have reflected greater commitment. Brad, by contrast, didn't want to allocate any more time to the relationship unless he was more certain of positive results.

Serena prevailed. However, they couldn't find a time to work on Chapter 4 together as she'd wished, and so kept separate notebooks.

Serena's notebook

- We've been separated and reconciled three times
- When I want to be with Brad, he wants a separation, and vice versa
- What's our issue??? Commitment?
- We don't fight so much as talk forever about whether to stay together
- The garbage [*the* fight] is about whether or not to stay together

Brad's notebook

- We hold each other back
- I want out before the kid remembers us together
- Serena wants to keep trying
- I think our problem is that we talk too much about it

Both notebooks end here. Without observations of specific interactions and the focus entailed in describing them, Brad and Serena were unable to identify any patterns of interaction or feelings that went with them. Additionally, they were unable to develop hypotheses about their relationship. And, without identifying the nature and dynamics of *the* fight, their chances for resolving it were greatly diminished.

Serena suggested they attempt to determine what their issue was, but Brad insisted the only problem was that they held each other back. Serena suggested they had a commitment problem, but Brad reassured her that if he were certain about the relationship he would have no problem staying in it.

Serena: We have a child now. Maybe it's time we decided to stay together and work on it.

Brad: I think we hold each other back.

Serena: Yeah, but how?

Brad: Well, just being together. You know, we come home from work, we have all sorts of expectations for each other, and then before we know it we've lost what we want for ourselves.

Serena: Don't you think that's what happens to some extent in all relationships?

Brad: No, I don't. We've never figured out how to let each other be ourselves.

Serena: How would you do that?

Brad: I'd ask myself, what do I want to do after work today? And you'd do the same.

Serena: And the baby?

Brad: As long as he's with us, he doesn't care.

Serena: We could see if it works.

Brad: When has it ever worked for us? It's only worked when we've been separated.

Serena: Are you sure?

Brad: Yes. I think if we were different people, if we didn't have so many expectations for each other, maybe it'd work.

Serena: You think there are couples with no expectations for each other?

Brad: Sure. Or fewer.

At this point, their discussion had veered into theory and away from identifying *the* fight. Additionally, when they talked about themselves, they focused on themselves as individuals, rather than as a couple. Thus, the impact of their interactions got lost.

Brad and Serena each lacked the degree of self-awareness needed to engage in this process. They were also ambivalent about commitment. I suspect each was unduly threatened by suggestions s/he contributed to the relationship malaise. Taken together, these characteristics suggested a need for professional intervention (Chapter 8).

Because Brad and Serena were unable to progress in identifying *the* fight in their relationship, analysis of their dialogue would not be productive in your quest to stop *the* fight in your own relationship. It is interesting from a professional perspective, but not for purposes of this book.

Conclusion

The four couples exemplify a range of approaches to identifying *the* fight in their relationships. Although two of them experienced difficulty, many couples will benefit from engaging in the exercises leading to identifying *the* fight and neither of the couples who experienced problems with the exercises were worse off for having attempted them.

It is now time for you to do the exercises in Chapter 4. If you've been unable to resist the temptation and have begun already, take a moment before you go on to Chapter 6. Think back over the work you've done so far, and once again savor your increased awareness. You have new skills, understandings, and behaviors at your disposal as you begin the culmination of your work: resolving *the* fight and getting rid of the garbage in your relationship.

Part III
Getting Rid of Your Garbage

6

Resolving *the* Fight and Getting Rid of the Garbage

Now it's time to transform your awareness about *the* fight in your relationship into options for resolving it. Although the reading and the exercises to identify *the* fight in your relationship (Chapter 4) were part of the process of increasing your options for change, you're now going to take direct action to transform your relationship.

Awareness precedes change. You can't change something if you don't know what it is. Identifying *the* fight was therefore a crucial step toward resolving it.

Here's an example. Saying, "I'm unhappy" conveys what you are feeling but provides minimal information about your situation. If asked, "And then what?" you might respond that you want to be happier. To know what to do to increase your happiness (or diminish your unhappiness), you must identify very specifically what it is that's making you unhappy. Saying, "I'm unhappy because I have to get up so early in the morning" helps. But, are you unhappy because you didn't get enough sleep, you're not looking forward to the day ahead, or you don't like to get up when it's still dark outside? If you didn't get enough sleep, then two more questions arise: did you have difficulty sleeping, or did you go to bed too late to wake up refreshed when your alarm rang? If you're not looking forward to the day, other questions occur, most importantly, what about your day bothers you? Is it your job, the monotony of your routine, coming home to a partner who enrages you? If you don't like getting up when it's dark outside, it might help to examine your emotional reactions to winter or ways to make your work schedule more flexible. And what do you mean by unhappiness?

Obviously, what you do about your unhappiness depends on the answers to these questions. There's no point looking for a new job if you need to go to bed an hour earlier—take it in 15-minute segments over the course of a week or two. On the other hand, there's no point in going to bed earlier if the problem is relationship distress. Identifying the source of your unhappiness allows you to see more clearly what you need to do to change it. Then you can decide whether and how to do it.

I believe this is the way change works. First, you identify the problem in as detailed a fashion as possible. Second, you examine your options for managing the problem. Third, you decide whether to act on any of these options and if so, which one(s). Fourth, you act. And finally, you assess whether your action resolved the problem and if not, or not completely, you adjust your action or act on your next option. So, the process of identifying *the* fight in your relationship, which you undertook in Chapter 4, will guide your change process.

Once you identify your options, you can begin to experiment with them. The first option for resolving *the* fight in your relationship may not work. That's why it's important to have several options.

Western thought leads us to view the world in terms of dichotomies, and in our own lives this plays out in the assumption that everything we do reflects either-or choices. We tend to think, either I'm happy or I'm unhappy. In reality, many more possibilities exist. You may be happy in some aspects of your life, although not in others. You may be happy some of the time, but unhappy at other times, for instance, when you've lost sleep. Most of us pay lip service to the idea that of course our relationship can't mirror a romance novel; there are always adjustments, etc. But, do we act like we believe our own press, or do we view the quality of our relationships as a dichotomy, either good or bad?

Your relationship may never be exactly what you want it to be, but that doesn't mean it can't be very, very good. If there are no options other than the relationship being the stuff of fairy tales or awful, then dealing with life as a couple becomes very difficult.

Your partner may be an intelligent person who happens to be very quiet in large social situations. Can you tolerate your acquaintances not knowing how intelligent s/he is? I would guess the answer is yes, as long as your relationship is otherwise fine. On the other hand, if these acquaintances judge your partner negatively, you may feel uncomfortable when you're all together and your discomfort may become problematic.

If you're thinking in dichotomies, your options are: get rid of your partner or get rid of the acquaintances. But, if you're thinking in terms of multiple options, you can spend less time with these acquaintances, not include your partner when you make plans with them, or tell them you don't appreciate whatever they do that leaves you feeling they don't value your partner. Then, you can choose which option best fits you and the particular situation, and try it out. If it doesn't work, adjust it or try another option.

This is how awareness leads to options, and how options then lead to change. As you go through the process of increasing your options and resolving *the* fight, remember that awareness is crucial to change. You might find it helpful to continue observing your interactions with your partner and using the identification techniques from Chapter 4. You might also benefit from reading the examples in Chapter 7 before you begin working on the exercises described in this chapter.

In this chapter, I'll provide you with some specific ideas and techniques to help you resolve *the* fight in your relationship. Think of these as tools. I'm also going to take you through a five-step process for identifying and enacting your options for resolving *the* fight and stopping the accumulation of garbage in your relationship.

There may be obstacles to change, within yourself, your partner, or the dynamic between the two of you. An important part of any assessment involves identifying these impediments and then deciding how to get around them.

If you were able to work with your partner on the exercises in Chapter 4, continue to work together. If you didn't work together on Chapter 4, you probably had a good reason. Unless you've re-thought your decision, you probably need to work alone on this chapter, as well.

Tools and Concepts

In this section, I'm going to address five key concepts and show you how to use them as tools as you engage in the process of changing your relationship. These five conceptual tools are:

- Metacommunication;
- Increasing empathy;
- Making the implicit explicit;
- Questioning assumptions;
- Getting unstuck and seeing your options when you and your partner have become polarized.

I have alluded to each of these concepts in previous chapters. Now it's time to fully explain them and show you how to use them as tools to improve your relationship.

Using these five tools will allow you to have *the* fight without accumulating more garbage. Rather, you can use these tools to work toward resolution of *the* fight in your relationship, so that the trash doesn't become *the* fight and then more garbage.

<u>Metacommunication</u>. Metacommunication involves communicating about communication. It's a very effective technique for stopping a negative interaction in its tracks. I used it when I said,

"This is *the* fight again, isn't it?" in the introduction. Once you have identified *the* fight in your relationship, you can use metacommunication in the same way to stop *the* fight.

In Chapter 4, Alan and Samantha used metacommunication during their argument about when he would take the lawn mower to be fixed. Samantha said, "I'd really like, just once, to talk about something that needs doing around here without fighting about whether you think I'm working enough." While *the* fight was not re-solved by this metacommunication, it stopped the argument from escalating into *the* fight by addressing the way in which they were communicating.

Acknowledging *the* fight allows you a range of alternatives to what you've already been doing. You've probably been using a com-bination of ignoring or avoiding *the* fight and battling ahead despite it. Alan and Samantha acknowledged that *the* fight was happening and then agreed to table it. As they demonstrated, acknowledging the wish to disengage from *the* fight can be a powerful tool. Ac-knowledging *the* fight diminished Alan and Samantha's anger and tension and allowed them to walk away from one another before *the* fight created more garbage. Again, this use of metacommunica-tion didn't resolve *the* fight; it did, however, stop the accumulation of more garbage.

A second option involves using metacommunication as a tool to resolve *the* fight. Samantha and Alan talked about how "...fight-ing about whether you [Alan] think I'm working enough" affects their relationship. This option addresses *the* fight about Saman-tha's work outside the home and how it manifests whenever they argue about anything.

Here's an example of how Alan and Samantha could meta-communicate about *the* fight and then move toward resolving it. First, however, let's review the argument as it moved into *the* fight.

Samantha [voice beginning to rise in volume and pitch]: We agreed you'd take the mower in to be fixed this weekend. It's up to you when you do it.

Alan [angry]: Well, I ran out of time. You're the one with all the time on your hands. You do it.

Samantha [angry]: When do you think I'd find the time? I don't have time to do everything you don't feel like doing. I work 30 hours a week and take care of everything for the kids and the house.

Alan [sarcastic]: You'll pardon me if I'm not interested in how hard you work.

Samantha [frustrated, voice rising in volume]: It's not about how hard I work, Alan. It's about *you* not doing things you say you'll do and then expecting *me* to do them as though I don't work at all. I'd really like, just once, to talk about something that needs doing around here without fighting about whether you think I'm working enough.

Alan [after a pause, voice soft]: Ok, Sam. Let's talk about the mower.

Alan chose to address the argument about the mower instead of *the* fight about how much Samantha worked outside the home. The argument about the mower was easier to resolve, being less entrenched than *the* fight about their covert contract that Samantha pursue a career and whether she was continuing to be a good spouse without a full-time career. Once they resolved the argument about the mower, they could then either move on to discuss *the* fight or agree to table that conversation for another time. By the way, this is a great example of how options multiply, once you begin to recognize them.

Samantha [also in a softer voice]: I would like to be able to count on you to do things when you say you will.

Alan: Yeah, I understand. But things come up. When I said I'd take the mower in, I didn't know about this thing at work.

Samantha: I'd rather you didn't say you'd do something unless you're willing to make time to do it.

Alan: [Hint of sarcasm returning to his voice] Oh, right…

Samantha: No, really. Tell me you're going to work and when you would make time.

Alan: Sometimes I don't feel I can say no or later to you.

Samantha: I really wish you would.

Alan: And I don't always think of it. Like this weekend. When I decided to go into the office yesterday, I didn't think about John having a game this afternoon.

Samantha: His schedule is on the refrigerator. You could look.

Alan: Yeah, but I'm not in the habit.

Samantha: Do you want me to remind you?

Alan: That would help.

Samantha: Really? If you say, "I'm going into the office today" on Saturday and I say, "Remember John has a game on Sunday and you promised to take the lawn mower to the shop", you won't get mad at me for nagging or trying to stop you from going to work?

Alan: No, especially not if I remember I asked you to remind me [smiles], which I just did.

Samantha: Ok, I'm willing to try it.

Alan: Good, because, you know, I could have dropped off the mower yesterday on my way into the office. I just didn't think.

Samantha: Ok. Good.

Alan and Samantha resolved the argument about the mower without getting lost in *the* fight about Samantha working outside the home. Had they reverted to *the* fight, their initial argument about the mower would have become part of the relationship garbage generated by yet another unresolved occurrence of *the* fight along with the trash about the mower not being resolved.

As they, and you, experiment with and then practice new ways of relating, additional arguments may emerge. If either of you can metacommunicate, these arguments can be resolved without devolving into *the* fight. If Samantha remembers to remind Alan that he asked her to remind him of what he's promised to do, then they can avoid being distracted by *the* fight when problems like taking the lawnmower to be fixed occur.

Their first solution, which arose from the discussion described above, may or may not work for them. If it doesn't, they can refer back to this discussion and look for more alternatives. They have many options; and, as long as they keep their eyes on the goal of finding a solution to the current problem, rather than becoming distracted by *the* fight, they'll continue to discover new alternatives as the need arises.

At the conclusion of this discussion, Alan and Samantha had the option to talk about *the* fight or table it for another time. They've done a lot of work already, and I'd suggest they wait. However, because it's never fun to talk about *the* fight, they might benefit from setting a time to discuss it. Couples usually feel more secure about postponing a talk about the unfinished business between them if they know they will return to it.

Samantha: I think we need to talk about our feelings about my job sometime. Maybe not now.

Alan: No, I think we've talked enough for today.

Samantha: Yeah. So when do you want to talk again?

Alan: We're both pretty tired on weeknights and there's a lot to do. What about next weekend? Sunday mornings seem to work well.

Samantha: Ok.

You can use <u>metacommunication</u> to resolve *the* fight in your relationship by using one or more of the following tools:

- Stating directly that *the* fight is occurring;
- Stating clearly what you think *the* fight is about (even if you and your partner have already agreed, it helps to repeat a statement of what *the* fight is about as part of metacommunicating);
- Talking clearly about the processes that lead to and intensify *the* fight (you've identified these in Chapter 4);
- Brainstorming about what you could do differently and how interacting and/or behaving differently might lead to a different outcome, either circumventing or resolving *the* fight;
- Recognizing when you've talked enough for the moment; and
- Scheduling a time to resume the discussion.

<u>Increasing Empathy</u>. Empathy involves listening to another's position, being open to viewing the world through her or his eyes, and understanding (though not necessarily agreeing with) how s/he views it. Phil and Lucy, in Chapter 2, exemplify the potential use of empathy.

Phil liked to be cuddled and pampered when he was sick and his partner, Lucy, wanted him to leave her alone. Phil could demonstrate his empathy by imagining what it would be like to want the world to go away, while Lucy could do so by envisioning what it would be like to want to be cared for and nurtured. Phil can leave Lucy alone when she's sick and she can pamper him when he's sick if they rely on empathy for the other, rather than their own experience, to inform their behavior.

The capacity for empathy develops in most people during the preschool years (3-5). Children learn empathy by modeling the adults around them. So, children who grow up in homes where empathy doesn't exist or is masked by violence, substance abuse, or a parent's mental illness may not acquire the capacity or skills involved in empathetic behavior. When one or both partners have not learned empathy, outside intervention may be necessary before *the* fight can be resolved (see Chapter 8).

Failure to acknowledge one's partner's views and feelings diminishes their legitimacy and risks leaving one's partner feeling invalidated. Lack of empathy on one person's part often results in the other's increasing her/his efforts to obtain it: If I just scream louder, s/he'll understand how important this is to me. But, if s/he truly can't understand that another's perspective could be different from her/his own, then screaming louder will not change anything and increasing frustration results. Additionally, each partner may come to believe that lack of empathy indicates lack of caring or respect.

Unresolved arguments and the accumulation of garbage tend to reduce empathy between partners, even when both are capable of it. Empathy requires attention to the other and receptiveness to her or his needs. In other words, empathy requires effort. Ill will between partners often decreases their motivation to work that hard.

However, partners can reclaim their empathy, either by resolving *the* fight and reducing the garbage between them, or by using empathy as a tool to achieve these goals. I recommend you work on increasing empathy as you attempt to resolve *the* fight, because it's an important tool that you may need at your disposal.

To increase your empathy, begin by concentrating on what your partner says and does. This is easier to do when you're getting along than during an argument. Think about what your partner might be experiencing. If s/he's staring into space, don't assume s/he's thinking about something just because you stare into space only when you're lost in thought. Rather, think about what you know about your partner. Perhaps s/he stares into space when s/he's bored. Ask your partner what's up. If s/he says, "I'm trying to figure out what to do", imagine what it's like to be thinking about what to do. If you find yourself getting angry because you've got a to-do list a mile long and you'd be happy to give her/him something other than staring into space to do, remind yourself that s/he's bored, rather than avoiding or disrespecting the importance of your to-do list. Then, you might ask her/him whether s/he'd be willing to help you with your list. Not only are you more likely to get a positive response with this approach, but also you're more likely to avoid an argument that leads to *the* fight and more garbage in your relationship.

Once you've practiced viewing your interactions with your partner more empathetically, you may find yourself feeling more compassion for your partner's perspective when s/he does those things that previously left you hurt and/or angry. Then, you can begin to use empathy to deflect *the* fight when you disagree.

When Samantha wrote in her notebook, "Alan thinks I work too little and I think I work too much", she expressed empathy for Alan's position in *the* fight between them, by acknowledging their different perspectives. While she disagreed vehemently with him, she gave his perspective validity by acknowledging its existence and the legitimacy of him viewing their situation differently than she does. Additionally, her empathy allowed her to disengage from the battle about whose position was reasonable, a prerequisite to change.

The following example illustrates how Samantha and Alan used empathy to help resolve *the* fight in their relationship. It's the weekend after their metacommunication about the lawn mower, and they'd agreed to talk about *the* fight about Samantha's work outside the home.

Alan: Where do we start?

Samantha: I'm not sure. I've been thinking that we're angry about different things, maybe too angry to listen to what the other is saying. So, we could start by saying what we're angry about, before we actually get angry.

This is a great idea. Stating the sources of their anger without the angry nonverbal messages may help them stay focused on the problem, rather than becoming distracted and responding to one another's anger instead.

Alan: Ok. I wrote in my notebook [pulls out notebook] that I miss your enthusiasm about work. And I'm frustrated with you because you're so involved with the kids.

Alan's statement about her involvement with the kids was phrased as an accusation, and he would have been wiser to focus only on missing Samantha's enthusiasm about work. In real life, Samantha might have become defensive about the extent of her involvement with the kids, for example, "You know I don't get to spend much time with them because I do work 30 hours a week," thus reigniting *the* fight. But instead, she used empathy to avoid becoming defensive.

Samantha: I never thought about you missing me. I was different before the kids were born, though, wasn't I?

Alan: Yes, you were. We used to have great times talking about work, listening to each other's ideas and accomplishments.

Samantha: I'm excited about the kids now. I wish you understood how much I love being a mother, being with them, taking care of them. It's much better than work; at least I feel it is.

Alan: Yeah, I don't understand how you can say that. And I guess I haven't been trying to understand it. I wanted you to stay the same, and I've been frustrated by your changes.

Samantha: I can understand you not wanting me to change. But I have. And when you act as though I've done something bad, I get angry with you. Can you at least recognize my perspective, even if you don't like it?

Alan: Yeah, ok. Remind me what your perspective is.

Samantha: Ok. I want to be at home with the kids. I love being a mother.

Alan: Ok, so you get angry at me for insisting you work when you want to be home with the kids?

Samantha: Yes, especially when you're angry with me for wanting to be home.

Alan: I think I understand. Now, can you recognize my perspective?

Samantha: Yes, that you miss how I used to be.

Samantha and Alan used a technique that can be extremely useful during couple misunderstandings. Each stated her/his understanding of the other's perspective, giving her/his partner the opportunity to concur, edit, or refute that understanding. In this way, couples can be sure they have arrived at an accurate understanding of one anothers' statements prior to responding.

At this point, Alan and Samantha began to strategize about how to keep some of what Alan so enjoyed about Samantha's enthusiasm for work in their relationship. They had several options. For example, they could spend the time talking about her work that they now spend fighting about whether she works outside the home. Or, they could hire a babysitter and go out to dinner on Fridays, at the end of the workweek, and talk about not only work but also other topics that generate enthusiasm for both of them. A third option would be to discuss the possibility of Samantha stopping work for awhile, whether it would be financially feasible, and whether she as a person and they as a couple would lose something of value if she did.

You can use increasing empathy as a tool in resolving *the* fight in your relationship by:

- Listening to your partner's verbal and nonverbal communications;
- Reflecting back what you hear and telling your partner you want feedback about whether you have heard him or her correctly;
- Listening to the feedback;
- Putting yourself in your partner's place. You can do this by imagining what s/he experiences (thinks and feels) based on what you already know about your partner. You can also put yourself in your partner's place by switching roles (you say what you think your partner would and s/he say what s/he thinks you would in your conversation);
- Adjusting what you say to your partner based on your awareness about how s/he receives it; and
- Recognizing when you are too angry, tired, or sad to be empathetic and suggesting you continue the conversation another time (be sure to tell your partner when).

Making the Implicit Explicit. You can try this very old therapy technique at home. Making the implicit, or hidden aspects of yourself and your relationship, explicit, or acknowledged, involves recognizing exactly what these implicit parts are. You can recognize the implicit by acknowledging what has not before been acknowledged. Specifically, you can begin to make what has been implicit now explicit by asking yourself, what am I really doing, thinking, feeling, or wanting and what are we, as a couple, really fighting about? Once you have an answer or answers, you can choose whether or not to express your new awareness to your partner.

Whatever is implicit exists, though not necessarily within your awareness. It's the subtext, the underlying theme of what you do. In relationship contracts, there is the explicit contract and the implicit one (11). In Samantha and Alan's relationship, part of the explicit contract was that they share responsibility. An aspect of the implicit contract for Alan was that Samantha would equally share financial responsibility, as well as responsibility for keeping their conversations interesting in a way that was important to Alan, by continuing to pursue her career. However, because this clause in their relationship contract was implicit and never talked about, Samantha had neither known about nor accepted it. Hence, *the* fight about this implicit clause ensued when the subject of her wanting to be a stay-at-home mom and everything related to it arose.

Just as *the* fight represents an issue that underlies almost all your disagreements, whatever is implicit underlies many of your behaviors, thoughts, and feelings. Recognition makes the implicit explicit; it's no longer hidden. And recognition, the catalyst for this conversion, can be a very powerful tool.

Therapists make the implicit explicit all the time, by simply stating what they hear their clients say that the clients have not previously noticed. When what the client is saying is implicit, or outside her or his awareness, making it explicit in this way creates the potential for change.

For example, a young woman in an advanced degree program for professionals while working at a full-time, professional job said she often does her assignments at the last minute.

> Marissa: They tell me I'm doing fine, but I know I'm cutting corners.

Marissa's explicit message describes her belief that her work is inadequate and the faculty members are somehow missing her deficiency. The implicit message is far more significant: Marissa doesn't trust that her own decisions about how she prioritizes schoolwork are valuable and expects to be criticized for them.

> Therapist: It sounds like you've prioritized your job and school in a way that works. You get your assignments done, and the people who are evaluating you think you're doing fine.

> Marissa: Well, yes.

> Therapist: Yet, you're anxious about how little time you spend on your schoolwork and about doing it at the last minute, as though you're pulling a fast one on the faculty. I'm puzzled that you feel this way even though your priorities are accomplishing your goals.

> Marissa: It sounds ridiculous when you say it, to be anxious when something is working.

By making Marissa's implicit anxiety explicit, her therapist helped her see that it is unwarranted in this situation.

Couples also can benefit from making the implicit explicit. Alan's sarcastic remarks about how little Samantha works implied displeasure without acknowledging it. His comments were implicit criticisms of Samantha's choice to work part-time. As unacknowledged disparagement, these remarks invariably led to an argument.

Alternatively, when Alan explicitly expressed his upset about Samantha's career choice after their children were born, he and Samantha had much more productive conversations. Listen to the difference between a dialogue in which Alan expressed implicit anger and one in which it was explicit.

> Alan [frustrated]: Well, I ran out of time. You're the one with all the time on your hands. You do it.

Alan's implicit anger appeared in his accusation that she was "… the one with all the time on [her] hands…."

> Samantha [angry]: When do you think I'd find the time? I don't have time to do everything you don't feel like doing. I work 30 hours a week and take care of everything for the kids and the house.

Samantha's response, which focused on defending herself regarding the demands on her time, demonstrated how difficult responding to implicit anger, or any unspoken message, can be. If it doesn't have a name, how does one address it?

In the following hypothetical excerpt, Alan expressed his anger explicitly. Notice how differently Samantha responded.

> Alan [frustrated]: Well, I ran out of time. It seems like you must have more time than I do, because you don't have to be in the office as much as I do. So, I don't think I should have to be late for John's game to take in the mower.

> Samantha [also frustrated]: You're right; I don't have to be in the office as much as you do. But I have a lot of responsibilities around here that you don't have, and I'd like you to take the time I spend taking care of the kids and the house into account when you start getting upset about how much time you think I have.

Alan's explicit statement about his anger didn't stop Samantha from getting angry herself. However, being explicit helped focus their conversation on a very important piece of *the* fight in their relationship. Recognizing the source of your frustration—in other words, making an implicit physiological response to frustration an explicit awareness of the source of the frustration—often affects your interactions with your partner in a positive way.

You can use making the implicit explicit as a tool to resolve *the* fight in your relationship by:

- Asking yourself whether you are bothered whenever you hear your voice, feel your body language, or experience your emotions as negative toward your partner;
- Asking yourself what is bothering you when the answer is yes;
- Describing your upset, at least to yourself and possibly to your partner, in as specific terms as possible (if you are going to tell your partner, be sure to avoid accusatory language); and
- Addressing what is bothering you, either by discussing it with your partner or changing your behavior to reduce your upset.

Questioning Assumptions. We all hold many assumptions about the world. We've learned these assumptions from our experience and from what others have taught us. Most of these assumptions lie beyond our awareness. Yet, they underlie a great deal of what we think, feel, believe, and do.

When their first child was born, Samantha assumed that Alan would happily support her desire to become a stay-at-home mom. Her assumption was based on her experiences, both as a child watching her own parents and as an adult observing her friends. Her mother stopped working when she got married and stayed home with Samantha and her brothers until they went to college. Many of her friends decided to stay home with their children, some at the prompting of their husbands and others with their husbands' agreement, however reluctant.

Alan, on the other hand, assumed that his and Samantha's relationship would not change after they had children.

Alan: We'd always said you were such a career woman you wouldn't want to give it up. I was stunned and didn't know what to make of it when you said you wanted to quit your job after your maternity leave ended.

Samantha: My feelings surprised me, too. But, there they were, and I wanted your support.

Wanted? Or expected?

Therapist: Samantha, I understand you wanted Alan's support. It sounds like you also expected it, maybe assumed he'd be ok with your decision.

Samantha: Oh, absolutely.

Therapist: And, Alan, it sounds like you assumed Samantha wouldn't be like her friends who gave up their careers after they had children.

Alan: Yes, I thought she was different.

Assumptions, being implicit, must be made explicit before they can be questioned. Imagine you are your own therapist and ask yourself what your assumptions about relationships going into your relationship were. Did you assume relationships would be easy, not require much work? Did you assume love would change those things about your partner you didn't like? Did you hold gender assumptions, such as the woman being responsible for holding a heterosexual relationship together? Did you assume that what you loved about your partner would never change, that s/he'd remain unchanged over the years? And did you assume that your partner would want to hear every negative thought or feeling you have about her/him so s/he could change for you?

Some assumptions, like the ones listed above, may not only need to be made explicit, but also questioned, adjusted, and perhaps outright rejected. Relationships seem to require a lot of work, in part because it's so difficult for two people to live intimately together. And love has never been known to change abusive behavior or resolve mid-life questions, nor even motivation to pick up wet towels from the bathroom floor. It would be wonderful, though unrealistic, to insist our partners change the things we don't like and keep all of what we love about them no matter where life takes them. And, finally, most people don't want to hear every negative thought you have about them; the short story is, tell your partner the important things you'd like to be different, emphasizing what you'd like her/him to do rather than what s/he's been doing that you don't like. Tell her/him you'd like to have 15 minutes to change clothes and unwind alone when you get home from work. Don't, however, tell your partner how annoying it is to watch her/him put the plates in the dishwasher before the silverware.

Other assumptions may be more workable. Did you assume you and your partner would share life's joys and sorrows? Did you assume that, with love and attention, your relationship would endure? Did you assume your partner would accept you for who you are? Did you assume s/he would continue to be as responsible, in the ways you both defined as indicative of responsible behavior, as when you met?

Once you've recognized your assumptions about relationships, you can begin to ask yourself questions about their usefulness. How are they working for you? How are they setting you up for disappointment and your partner for failure? What other problems are they causing? Are they important to you? If so, how important are they to you?

Therapist: I have a question for each of you. Let's start with you, Alan. I'm curious how you thought Samantha would avoid the path her friends took after their kids were born.

Alan: I don't know. She seemed so committed to her career.

Therapist: What did she think of her friends' choice to stay home?

Alan: I thought she agreed with me that they were making a mistake, but maybe not. Maybe she said something about thinking they'd get bored.

Therapist: So she never said, "That's not for me," or, "I'd go crazy at home with a baby," or, "What's she thinking?"

Alan: No, she didn't. Are you suggesting maybe I jumped to a conclusion here? Because if you are, I think you're wrong. Samantha and I always talked about her continuing to work after we had kids.

Samantha: I *am* continuing to work.

Alan: I mean, like you did before. [To therapist] I guess maybe I assumed wrong, but I assumed.

Therapist: Now, Samantha, I'm curious what Alan did to lead you to assume he'd be happy about whatever decision you made about staying home with children?

Samantha: Well, nothing, obviously. I just thought that's what husbands do.

Note that neither Samantha nor Alan sound particularly happy to have their assumptions questioned. However, it's usually more helpful to question your own, rather than your partner's assumptions, since you have the power to change your own assumptions while it's your partner's choice to change hers/his. In other words, let your partner question her/his own.

You can use <u>questioning assumptions</u> by:

- Listing the assumptions you have about relationships and, if possible, asking your partner to do the same with respect to her/his assumptions;
- Asking yourself which of your assumptions are working;
- Asking yourself whether any of your assumptions are hurting your relationship; and
- Asking yourself whether your assumptions are realistic.

<u>Getting Unstuck When You and Your Partner Have Polarized</u>. In <u>The Tao of Physics</u>, Fritjof Capra (17) described the polarization of western thought, culminating with the work of Descartes. Descartes and almost three centuries of western scientists and philosophers who followed him viewed mind and body as dichotomous categories, i.e., having no overlap. Over the years, the duality between mind and body became more extreme.

Social science writers of the 19th and 20th centuries developed dialectical theories to describe, for example, social and economic behavior and human development (18, 19). These theories hold that two opposing forces exist. When one is chosen, the individual or social group is able to move on to a higher level of development. When the other is chosen, they remain stuck and subsequent stages cannot be successfully undertaken. Notice that there is a right-wrong component to these categories, and success is contingent upon making the correct choice.

A relevant dialectical theory is the developmental theory of Erik Erikson (20). In his theory, adolescents confront the task of developing an identity; failure results in lack of a cohesive sense of self. When the individual develops an identity, s/he is prepared to assume the next developmental task, that of creating an intimate relationship. When her or his identity remains diffuse, s/he cannot successfully create an intimate relationship.

Erikson's developmental theory provides an example of the polarization that results from viewing the world in terms of dichotomies. Are there no alternatives to having an identity or having no (diffuse) identity? I think there are. Some people are very focused on a career goal, but have not thought through how they view themselves as part of a couple. Others have a clear idea of what they want their personal lives to look like, but have not yet found their career path. Still others know who they are professionally and interpersonally, but have not yet developed a realistic body image and see themselves as less attractive than they are.

Viewing the two categories in these dichotomies as two ends of a continuum provides you with more options. Once you begin to view your life as existing along such continua, rather than as a series of dichotomies, then you can shift your focus away from the extremes, or ends. At that point, you can more easily see that you have numerous alternatives available to you between the extremes and that your choices are not dichotomous.

On a relationship level, viewing dichotomies as endpoints of a continuum allows you to stop polarizing your arguments with your partner into good/bad, right/wrong, and other either/or scenarios and instead look for options that lead to resolution. For example, if *the* fight in Samantha and Alan's relationship cannot be resolved by determining who is right and who is wrong, then they can empathize with each other's viewpoints and begin to look for options that may be more acceptable to both of them.

I believe that as people repeat *the* fight in their relationship over and over again, their positions become not only more entrenched but also more extreme. These extreme positions can be conceptualized as the poles of a continuum and may look like a dichotomy.

Once you get unstuck from the notion of all-or-nothing, the range of options becomes theoretically infinite, limited only by your creativity and how quickly you arrive at an alternative that works for you. I've found that, as couples explore their options, their positions generally become less extreme and the tone of their interactions softens.

When you notice that you and your partner have taken extreme positions, or polarized, you then have any number of options, or choices, along the continuum that connects these poles. At least one of these options is likely to be palatable to both of you, whereas if there are only two choices the probability of agreeing plummets.

Alan and Samantha have polarized over *the* fight in their relationship about Samantha working outside the home. She wants to be home with the children, and Alan wants her to resume her full-time career. However, they have other options, including the one they are enacting, in which Samantha works 30 hours per week. She could also work half time. Or, she could find a way to use her skills, training, and experience to work for herself, possibly even at home, and thus have a more flexible schedule and be able to spend more time with her children. Alan and Samantha are both professionals making reasonable incomes. They might also consider paying for the some of services around the house that currently fall to Samantha, so she has more time with their children when she's not at work and they both feel less burdened. These are only some of the options between the extremes, or dichotomy, of resuming her former job full-time or becoming a stay-at-home mom.

> Alan: Look, neither of us is happy with our situation. You're angry about working so much, and I'm angry that you don't work more. We could go on fighting about you staying at home or working full-time forever, but maybe we could look at whether there's a way to make us both happier.

Samantha: Ok. I guess it couldn't get much worse than it is now, as long as you're willing to consider options besides me working full-time.

Alan: Yeah, I am. I've been thinking about this, and as much as I'd like you to, you're not going to be happy working full-time while the kids are growing up.

Samantha: No. And I think you want me to be more enthusiastic about work, so we can have fun with it again, right?

Alan: Right.

Samantha: Ok, well I've been thinking, too, and I think if I were doing something else I might get excited about it. I think doing less of my same old job has made me less enthusiastic about it. I'd like to look for another job, a part-time professional job. And if I can't make that happen, my friend Patsy at work knows someone who job shares, and I was thinking that might help, because I'd have a close working relationship with the person I shared a job with, and being with colleagues is one of the things I miss not working full-time.

Alan: I don't know about all that. Would you work less?

Samantha: Yeah, probably half time. I know it'd be less money, but it's not like staying home. I'd still be earning money.

Alan: I don't know. I worry about how we're going to get these kids through college, and the less you earn the less we save.

Samantha: Yeah, but if I were happier we'd be happier, and it's not like I wouldn't be earning anything. I understand that my being a stay-at-home mom isn't going to work for us, much as I'd like it to.

Alan: You're right, Sam. It's not. But I guess returning to your old career isn't going to work   either?

Samantha: Right, Alan. It's not. At least not now.

Alan and Samantha will not resolve *the* fight in their relationship in one discussion. However, they used both empathy and getting unstuck from their previous polarization to make good progress exploring their options for change.

You can use <u>getting unstuck when you and your partner have polarized</u> by:

- Viewing the positions you and your partner have taken as two extreme ends of a continuum of options;
- Shifting your focus from the poles, or ends, to the continuum which connects them;
- Using your creativity to find options along the continuum;
- Working with your partner to agree on options that could work for both of you; and
- Rethinking your options as often as necessary to find one that works well for you as a couple.

<u>Conclusion</u>. As you move through the five-step process for resolving *the* fight in your relationship, remember to use the five tools in your conversations with your partner. These tools are:

- Metacommunication;
- Increasing empathy;
- Making the implicit explicit;
- Questioning assumptions;
- Getting unstuck and seeing your options when you and your partner have polarized.

Resolving The Fight in Your Relationship: A 5-Step Process

The time has arrived to work on resolving *the* fight in your relationship, by exploring and enacting your options. Take the time
to read the remainder of this chapter, as well as the next chapter, before beginning. I've designed these readings to help you
through the process; so don't wait till you're finished to read them.
I also encourage you to refer back to any part of this book, as well
as your notebook, as needed.

The five steps you'll use to resolve *the* fight are:

* Naming your goal, outcome, or change;
* Listing options for approaching the outcome you want;
* Prioritizing your options and choosing a place to start;
* Enacting and experimenting with your options;
* Assessing the outcome of your enactments and making
  adjustments.

The first three steps in this five-step process of resolving *the*
fight and stopping the accumulation of garbage in your relationship focus on identifying your options. The final two steps involve
enacting these options.

If you did the exercises in Chapter 4 with your partner, work
together again. If you did them separately or alone, it's probably
best to work the same way on the following exercises.

Step 1: Naming Your Goal, Outcome, or Change. When you
identified *the* fight in Chapter 4, you named your problem. Now it's
time to name your solution.

What is your goal for your relationship? What would you like
the outcome of reading this book to be for you and your partner?
What would you like your relationship to look like? Be like? Where
would you like you and your partner to be in terms of your relationship in a year? In 5 years?

I'm not much for 5-year plans. Life and people change in unpredictable ways, and so these plans appear to set people up for disappointment. However, envisioning what you'd like the future to be provides information about what you want right now, and that is what my questions about where you'd like you and your partner to be then are intended to uncover.

Awareness, once again, is essential to identifying options. Be aware of what you want the resolution of *the* fight in your relationship to look like, and then your path to change, or options, will become clearer.

When you identified *the* fight, you looked at the part(s) of your relationship that bring(s) you unhappiness. Naming the outcome you seek helps shift your focus to those aspects of your relationship that bring you joy.

You may remember a time when you were nicer to each other. Include the behaviors you associate with niceness in your goals. Or, there may be some new characteristic you'd like to be part of your relationship.

Get out your notebook and create a section called "Name my Outcome" or "Name my Goal". Now, brainstorm on paper. This section of your notebook is a wish list. Be as creative, yet specific as possible. One or more of these three prompts might help you.

- Paint a picture of how you'd like you and your partner to relate to one another. Place special attention on how you'd like to relate around the issue we've been calling *the* fight in your relationship.
- Imagine you could wave a magic wand. What would be changed in your relationship?
- Describe an ideal day with you partner. How would you avoid *the* fight?

You can also use the following questions to prompt a description of your desired outcome.

- What is your goal for your relationship?
- Where would you like it to be in a year? 5 years?
- What would you like your time with your partner to look like? Be like?
- What from the past that perhaps you've lost would you like to bring back into your relationship?
- What have you never had that you'd like to be part of your relationship now?
- How would you like to work together to make necessary adjustments when life demands them?

Be sure you're including a change in yourself and the way you relate, as well as in your partner. Samantha writing that a perfect day would involve Alan joyfully going off to work while she remained at home with the children isn't a realistic goal. Neither is Alan writing that Samantha would return to work full-time and then they'd spend evenings talking about their careers. If she worked full-time, they'd spend their evenings frantically supervising homework, preparing and cleaning up after dinner, and getting ready to repeat the whole thing the next day. They'd also spend evenings negotiating childcare when one or the other needed to travel.

After you've described your desired outcome, or named your goal, list the changes involved in achieving it. For example, Samantha might say that Alan recognize she cannot earn as much as a full-time career woman or do as much as a stay-at-home mother when she does neither full-time. Concomitantly, Alan might write that both he and Samantha find peace with the balance she has chosen and no longer feel tense and angry with one another about it. This would free them to problem solve about taking the lawn mower to be fixed, for example, without fighting about Samantha's allocation of time between work and home and their upset with one another about it.

Here are Alan and Samantha's entries.

Samantha's notebook

If I could wave a magic wand, I'd want us to be close again. We'd like each other, treat each other well (talk nicely to each other), be happy to see each other, and be able to talk and plan without fighting. He'd be happy for me that I enjoy being with the kids and see the advantages of me not working full-time. I guess I'd need to work, so it'd be ½-time. We'd go out sometimes, just the two of us, and I wouldn't mind because I'd be home more during the week. We'd laugh together and appreciate each other like we used to. We'd be more romantic with each other, maybe not like when we were first together, but we'd remember we're attracted to each other and want to do nice things for each other sometimes and touch and kiss. And we'd be partners. We'd make decisions together, without fighting. And we'd respect each other.

Alan's notebook

We'd like each other and not fight. Sam would probably not work full-time, but she'd stop complaining about it. And we'd have more sex. We'd spend time together and do things without the kids, like go to movies. We'd laugh. And she'd probably want us to share the work around the house more. I need more time to myself, so maybe we'd trade: I'd give her time alone and she'd give me time alone. I'd like to look forward to seeing her at the end of the day.

I'm impressed with how similar Alan and Samantha's entries were. While they worded them differently, they both talked about enjoying one another's company, finding a way for each of them to be content with Samantha's balance of work and home, and regaining the romantic, sexual part of the relationship.

If you're working on this project with your partner, compare your entries and pick out the similarities. The wording need not be identical. Look for meanings. Also look for places where your goals are similar enough to achieve a solution that would make you both happy. For example, Samantha wrote of wanting to spend time together and laughing, while Alan talked of doing things together. Both involved time with each other. Similarly, Samantha talked of romance and attraction, while Alan wrote about sex. Look for ways like these in which you and your partner's dreams are close enough that you can both achieve what you want by taking similar action.

Step 2: Listing Options for Approaching the Outcome You Want. Now that you're aware of what you want, it's time to decide how to get there. For each goal, outcome, or change you listed in Step 1, list three possible ways to achieve it in a section of your notebook called "Options".

Brainstorm. Use the tools and what you've learned from your observations in Chapter 4. Read the remainder of this chapter and Chapter 7 to get ideas from the four couples.

From their notebook entries, Alan and Samantha agreed on three outcomes:

- Enjoying one another's company,
- Finding a way for both to be content with Samantha's balance of work and home, and
- Regaining the romantic, sexual part of their relationship.

They then listed several options to attain each of these goals.

What are three ways Alan and Samantha could approach the goal of enjoying one another's company? First, they could take Kathy's (their first couple therapist) advice and spend more time enjoying themselves together. Alan listed movies, and Samantha suggested talking. I recommend going to a movie and then somewhere they can talk about the movie or anything else afterward, so they each get what they want. Without the children, obviously. How often do they need to do this: once a week, every other week, or once a month? Perhaps they need to limit the amount of time they spend together at first, something I recommend for couples whose relationships have become very distant and/or conflicted. They could go for a walk after dinner for 30 minutes to start. Then out for coffee for an hour. And finally, they could spend an entire afternoon or evening together.

Second, Alan and Samantha could agree to talk only about things they used to enjoy talking about. Examples might include the movie they just saw, politics, projects each was doing at work or separately at home, and their future.

A third option would be to find something new they could both enjoy doing together. They could take a woodworking or dance class together. They could volunteer time to an organization they agree does important work. They could get season tickets to a local theater company.

Their second goal, finding a way for both to be content with Samantha's balance of work and home, is more daunting. Samantha and Alan had polarized: Samantha wanted to be at home full-time and Alan wanted her to be at work full-time. Although they were beginning to negotiate, the question remained: Where was the point of reconciliation?

Since neither was going to get exactly what s/he wanted, they needed to agree on three options that each could live with. They were already living with a balance of Samantha working 30 hours each week. She was unhappy, not only because she wanted to spend more time at home with her children but also because she felt pressured to assume as much home care as if she were a stay-at-home mother. Meanwhile, Alan felt financially pressured and without enough time to contribute at home. So, this option wasn't working very well.

Could they both live with the option of Samantha working ½-time? This would give her more time at home and perhaps take some home care pressure off each of them. However, it would put a bigger financial burden on Alan. Could he live with this option?

Another option would be for Alan and Samantha to change their lifestyle to accommodate Samantha working less without pressuring Alan more. If they lived in a smaller house, stopped buying work clothes for Samantha, and didn't have child care expenses, could they make it financially with her at home? And, did she do the kind of work she could return to if she wanted or they needed more income? What would Alan get out of these changes? This option would require them to work cooperatively together.

Are you getting a sense of how identifying options works? Let's go on to Samantha and Alan's third goal: regaining the romantic, sexual part of their relationship. Some options include: agreeing to hug and kiss each other at least twice a day; arranging for their children to go to friends' houses to sleep and then going out for a romantic dinner and/or movie followed by a sexual encounter without fear of interruptions; and going away for a weekend together, perhaps to a place that holds happy memories for them.

Samantha and Alan's options were limited only by their imagination. And so are yours. You know yourself and your partner far better than I do. Even if you were my therapy clients, I'd be asking you for your suggestions about what might best work for you at this point in your relationship. The only two restrictions on your brainstorming are:

- Take it slowly if you've been very angry with one another for a long time; and
- Choose options you can agree on as you move to steps 4 and 5.

Step 3: Prioritizing Your Options and Choosing a Place to Start. Step 3 is relatively straightforward and simple. Take your lists of at least 3 options for each change, goal, or outcome you included in Step 1, and put those options in the order in which they seem most doable to you. Organize your priorities in your notebook in a section called, "Prioritizing My Options".

The order in which you prioritize your options can be based on what seems least difficult or most important to you. Or, there may be an intrinsic order to your options. Harris and Sherblom (20) suggested a 3-step model for organizing the results of brainstorming: put the options that seem most important and/or doable in pile A, the ones that seem impossible and/or unimportant in pile C, and those that don't fit either category into pile B. Then revisit B and place each idea in A or C. Although it's a good idea to keep both resulting piles, begin prioritizing within category A only. This process may help you if your list of options appears difficult to prioritize.

Alan and Samantha's options for regaining the romantic, sexual component of their relationship followed a logical progression, from affection through a single romantic and sexual encounter to a longer span of time together. Enacting their options in this order would allow them to gradually adjust to being together in ways they'd ignored for some time.

If your options contain no logical order, ask yourself what you believe you can undertake right now. Change is difficult, so all of your options may seem daunting. If so, pick one you think you could do if you push yourself. In other words, begin with the least difficult option.

Alternatively, one of your options may stand out as most important. If you find you must, you'll settle for one of the other options, but you'd prefer this one. I suspect Samantha might decide staying home with her children is so important that she'd like to begin with the option to change their lifestyle to accommodate her wish without overwhelming Alan. I also suspect that if she thought through this option, she might decide that cutting back to ½-time work is more doable, and start there. If Alan were involved in this decision, he might endorse this less drastic change.

If you listed more than one goal or change in Step 1, then you had more than one set of options in Step 2, i.e., a set of options for each goal. You need to prioritize your goals, as well as your lists of three options within each set. Again, use the criterion of either how important or how doable each change you wish to make appears, or whether a logical order to the changes you desire emerges. Samantha and Alan might prioritize their spending time together over changing their lifestyle, so that they would be better disposed toward each other before tackling Samantha's career options.

Here's a brief example from Samantha's notebook to help guide you.

Samantha's notebook

Prioritizing My Options

Enjoy each other (goal)

1. Go out for coffee together and don't talk about chores or me working
2. Go to a movie together and don't talk about chores or me working
3. Find something new to do together and do it

Romance and sex (goal)

1. Touch each other affectionately whenever we think of it
2. Kiss each other hello and good-bye
3. Go out to dinner on an evening the kids are at friends' houses and then spend time together alone afterward—don't talk about chores or me working

Balance work and home (goal)

1. Look at our finances and decide whether I could work ½-time
2. Look at our finances and figure out what we would have to change for me to stay home
3. Decide whether it's worth it

I'd like Samantha to be a bit more specific—how often will they do each activity listed under "enjoy each other" and "romance and sex"? Will they decide whether it's worth it to change her work-home balance together, or was she viewing the decision as hers alone? And what about Alan? Did she expect him to do less home and child care if she worked less outside the home? Would he have more time for his individual projects? If he needed to earn more money or they needed to change their lifestyle, how could he or they do this? Would he be willing to do it?

Samantha's decision to put balancing work and home last on her list may be crucial to its success. Once she and Alan are enjoying one another more, by spending time together doing things they enjoy and reclaiming the romance in their relationship, they'll find resolving *the* fight much easier.

Once you have your options ordered, you're ready to begin the final two steps in the process of resolving *the* fight and getting the garbage out of your relationship. These are enacting and experimenting with your options and assessing the outcome and making adjustments.

Step 4: Enacting and Experimenting With Your Options. Refer to your prioritized list of options from Step 3. Begin with the first option you've written under the first outcome, goal, or change on your list.

Now, use the five tools described earlier in this chapter, as well as any other form of communication between you and your partner that has been helpful to you in the past, to enact the first option. Remember, the five tools are:

- Metacommunication
- Increasing empathy
- Making the implicit explicit
- Questioning assumptions
- Getting unstuck and seeing your options when you and your partner have polarized

Before you begin to enact and experiment with your options, be sure to read through the remainder of this chapter and the examples in Chapter 7. These readings will finish preparing you to enact your own options for resolving *the* fight and getting rid of the garbage in your relationship.

Take your options one at a time. After each action, go on to Step 5, to assess and revise, before continuing to the next option. Steps 4 and 5 are interrelated, and you'll probably need to go back and forth between them.

Samantha: Let's plan to go out for coffee on Sunday afternoon and not get angry.

Alan: I'm pretty skeptical about this, Sam. The book says to do it, but I don't know whether it'll work.

Samantha: Yeah, I'm nervous, too. I guess we could plan what we'll talk about.

Alan: That's a bit stiff.

Samantha: Well, suggest something else.

Alan: I don't know. What'd we used to talk about?

In this dialogue, Alan and Samantha made the implicit—their concerns about spending time together without fighting—explicit and worked together to find possible solutions. They thus increased their options.

They also maintained empathy for one another's worry about their "date". Had one of them snapped at the other for her or his anxiety, they wouldn't have arrived at the point of identifying options to reduce their worry. So, their conversation became a shared, rather than an adversarial, experience, which bodes well for their "date".

Lastly, Alan and Samantha did a fantastic job of getting unstuck from the poles of either fighting or avoiding being alone together. Since they did this in a loving and open way, they arrived at an important question: "What'd we used to talk about?" The answer illuminated a place between the extremes of avoidance and conflict, thus allowing for the possibility of going out together and avoiding *the* fight.

Here's another example, this one from their third goal. Samantha initiated again, because this particular topic was far more important to her than to Alan.

> Samantha: I'd really like to look at our finances and decide whether we can afford for me to either cut back to 20 hours a week at work or stay home altogether.

If Alan and Samantha had lost trust for one another, Alan could feel set up by Samantha's opening line. She'd wanted to stop working outside the home all along, and he could conclude that she'd orchestrated changes in their relationship in order to get to this point. That's why balancing work and home was the third goal on Samantha's priorities list. Enjoying one another's company more and increasing the romance and sexuality in their relationship predisposed them to achieve more success as they addressed this far more difficult issue, *the* fight in their relationship.

> Alan: Is that what this has all been about?

He made what he believed was Samantha's implicit agenda to stop working explicit. Doing so permitted them to talk about it.

> Samantha: No. I bought the book to figure out how to get along better. And I admit I hoped I could get you to see the advantages of me being at home more. But at that time I wouldn't have considered working ½-time as an option or thought about your feelings.

Samantha demonstrated empathy for Alan's financial concerns in this statement.

> Alan: Ok. I want to believe you.

> Samantha: Good. I'm glad.

> Alan: So how do we do this?

Samantha: I'm not sure. You know more about our finances than I do. Do you have any idea about how we might figure this out?

Alan and Samantha were now positioned to look for options regarding whether they could afford Samantha working less outside the home. The details of how they proceeded from here are not as relevant as the tools they used to arrive at this point.

There are many more examples in Chapter 7 from the experiences of the four couples we've been following. First, though, let's review the final step in the process of resolving *the* fight and removing the garbage from your relationship.

<u>Step 5: Assessing the Outcome and Making Adjustments</u>. Did your enactment of your first option for your first goal in Step 4 work? Did you move toward your objective, or change what you identified in Step 1? If your answers to these two questions are unequivocally yes, then go on to the next goal in your priority list.

If your answer to either question was no, or even somewhat, you may need to modify the option or enact one of the other options to achieve that goal. And if the answers to the same questions regarding other options associated with this or other goals on your list are either no or somewhat, you also may find it helpful to tweak these other options, continue to the next option, or brainstorm more options, as well. We learn as much from what doesn't work as we do from what works, so please view the need for adjustments as an opportunity, rather than as a sign of failure. Remember, these enactments are experiments, or working hypotheses (Chapter 4). You may need to adjust and then repeat them, sometimes more than once, to achieve the outcome you want.

Ask yourself three questions:

- What, if anything, was not effective enough (didn't work or didn't work well)?
- What, if anything, got in the way, or blocked, my/our success?
- Do I/we need to adjust my/our strategy?

Perhaps your anger got in the way of clearly expressing your empathy. Do you need to add a step to more fully pave the way to your goal by addressing that anger in a way that prevents it from undermining your verbal and nonverbal messages to your partner?

We left Samantha and Alan examining their finances and deciding whether Samantha could either work less or stop working outside the home altogether. They were doing well, but could quite easily derail.

Alan: Well, it looks like we could afford for you to work ½-time if we gave up saving and cut about $100 per month from our spending.

Samantha: I think it'd be worth it for a while.

Alan: I don't know about not saving. What if something happened to my job? Or we had a big expense?

Samantha [frustrated]: It's not like we have no savings.

Alan [angry]: Yeah, and we've got two kids to educate and I'd like to retire before I drop dead of exhaustion.

Samantha [placating]: I think you're worrying too much about the future. I'd like to try living in the present more.

Alan [sarcastic]: Easy for you to say. You're practically retired now. And thanks for thinking about what you not working does to me.

Here comes *the* fight again. As Samantha became excited about the possibility of being at home with her children, her empathy for the impact of the proposed change on Alan diminished and her frustration with his arguments against her being home more increased. Alan, not surprisingly, responded with frustration and anger of his own. Empathy and then cooperation disappeared, and *the* fight resumed.

I suspect that once they began to seriously discuss an outcome Samantha wanted, she became excited that Alan might agree to it. But, clearly, there were difficulties with this option. Understandably, Alan expressed reluctance to agree to Samantha working less outside the home, as he did not see any benefit to himself or the family but rather more financial stress and potential difficulties for the family. Alternatively, Samantha enthusiastically offered to exchange some financial security for more time at home with her children. Without her empathy for his concerns or his for her enthusiasm, the conversation easily derailed and *the* fight ensued. Additionally, their positions became more extreme, or polarized.

At this point, Alan and Samantha could have agreed to take a break and resume their conversation at another time. If they suspended the discussion, they needed to set another, specific time to resume it. Samantha might have reviewed what happened, even recreating it in her notebook, and recognized that she needed to empathize with Alan. Alan might have done the same. Or, they could have practiced metacommunication and concluded that they needed to stop and rethink what they were doing whenever either sensed Samantha beginning to push for an agreement and/ or Alan beginning to resist her.

Alan and Samantha began to soften toward one another while doing the exercises in Chapter 4. By the time they reached the phase of enacting their options to achieve their goals, their relationship was already in better shape than it had been. They were both more aware of *the* fight and committed to resolving it, getting rid of the garbage, and returning to the relationship they'd once had. There was already far less ill will in their relationship, although tension remained just beneath the surface.

Not every couple can accomplish this level of success so quickly. If something impeded your progress toward actualizing one or more of your goals, even though you enacted and even tweaked all your options, ask yourself: was my partner or I too angry to enact the option? Was either of us unreceptive to either the option or to the other one of us? Do I/we need to examine more options, or are we stuck? If you're stuck, then your next step is to set the goal of becoming unstuck and explore and enact options to achieve it.

If you need to add goals or options or make adjustments to the ones you have, do so and then repeat the enacting, assessing, and adjusting cycle until you have reached your desired goal, outcome, or change. Do this before continuing. Then, when your goal is accomplished, you can move on to the next goal.

I'm suggesting a tremendous amount of work. You may find that *the* fight is more or less resolved and the accumulation of garbage halted long before you finish your list.

Since the purpose of engaging in this process was to resolve *the* fight and thus prevent the accumulation of more garbage in your relationship, you may decide to stop this process once *the* fight is resolved. That's fine. Finishing your entire list may be not only daunting, but also unnecessary.

Keep the list and your notebook, though. Then you can refer to them if you need to in the future. Life is a process, and change is inevitable. Your relationship will undoubtedly be affected by what you encounter in your future. You can return to the methods you've learned and used to identify and resolve future disagreements in your relationship, in other words, to prevent another fight from developing, if the need arises. You can also use these methods should events trigger a re-emergence of *the* fight in your relationship.

You've learned a way of viewing your relationship and actively working to improve it. Hopefully, what you've accomplished will help you deal with whatever changes you encounter along life's path. As with other exercises, take a moment to review your success and congratulate yourself on the effort you have put into bettering your relationship. You and your partner deserve not only praise for accomplishing what you've accomplished but also some time to savor the positive changes you've made.

7

Stories About Couples and Their Options

In this chapter, I'll describe how the four couples we've been following discovered options for resolving *the* fight in their relationships and getting rid of the garbage. They won't all succeed, and we'll revisit those who don't again in Chapter 8.

Alan and Samantha: Getting Rid of the Garbage

Alan and Samantha continued to review their options and reactions to one another about Samantha's work outside the home. They used metacommunication to avoid resuming *the* fight. The longer they talked without slipping into *the* fight, the more empathy they were able to generate. Samantha began to see the enormity of what she was asking of Alan and to understand how he might react, both to her and about what she was asking of him, as a result. And Alan, for his part, became more aware of the stress on Samantha of working outside the home as many hours as she did while taking on most of the responsibility for their home and children.

As their empathy for one another increased, their anger diminished. Alan paid more attention to honoring his promises to Samantha. He also took on more tasks around the house. As Samantha's anger at Alan decreased, she began to consider the possibility that she would not wish to be home forever. So, she began thinking about what she would like to do.

One evening when they were out to dinner, Samantha broached the subject.

Samantha: Listen, Honey. I've been thinking a lot and we've been talking a lot, which I really appreciate. And I have two suggestions. Ok?

Alan [openly, yet with a hint of suspicion]: I'm listening.

Samantha: I've begun to realize I won't want to be home forever. And I think I understand your concerns about what it would do to our financial situation if I stopped working. So, what I'd like to do is explore some possibilities besides what I'm doing now. I might not make as much money, at least at first, but I'd be earning something. And I really don't think I want to go back to what I've been doing full-time. For one thing, I'm now on the mommy track. But for another, the demands are too great. I need something that will challenge me without consuming me, because I want energy left over for other things.

She went on to tell him more specifically about the career change she was contemplating.

Alan and Samantha's situation illustrates how resolving *the* fight can lead to a lessening of garbage. The ill will between them evaporated as they listened empathetically to one another and worked together to find options to resolve *the* fight in their relationship. Once they stopped igniting *the* fight when they talked, they started feeling better about one another, enjoying their time together, and building good will. And when talking generated positive outcomes rather than another iteration of *the* fight, the garbage that had threatened to bury their relationship dissolved.

Adele and John: Resolving The Fight

Adele and John experienced a great deal of success working together to identify *the* fight in their relationship. They used two of the five tools (Chapter 6) quite effectively: metacommunication and making the implicit explicit.

John expressed his need for more empathy from Adele with clarity and precision. While Adele asked for a return to their status quo, she avoided accusing him of not caring about her and her feelings. In fact, it was his empathy for her pain that tended to derail him from asserting his own needs, leading him to regret decisions and concessions he'd made in the past.

Adele and John still needed to get unstuck from the polarized positions in which they found themselves. John recognized how much he'd accommodated Adele's need to placate her mother and sisters. He insisted that working with Mike in the town near them was the only way he could meet his current goals, one of which was avoiding a repetition of his tendency to adjust his needs to Adele's and to the demands of her mother and sisters. Adele, on the other hand, viewed staying away from her family of origin as the only option they had with which she could be happy. John and Adele's polarization around the issue of where to live led them to overlook a third option: lowering their cost of living so that John could work at a slower pace while Adele retained the opportunity to begin something new, possibly necessitating a move but not necessarily one which brought them closer to her mother and sisters.

They also needed to question their assumptions about each other. They both viewed Adele as needing rescuing; *the* fight was about whether or not John continued to accept that challenge as his responsibility. Similarly, they both viewed John as a rescuer, making it difficult for him to change his behavior. They had not yet addressed the question of what new roles they would assume to replace John as rescuer and Adele as needing to be rescued. It was this question that brought them around to naming a goal or outcome, the first step in the change process.

Adele and John continued to work together on the exercises in Chapter 6. In Step 1, they agreed to work toward the goal of making decisions based on their own needs, before anticipating what Adele's mother's reaction might be.

A potential pitfall of this goal was that John appeared to have already achieved it. So, the entire burden of change seemed to fall on Adele. Setting a goal that one partner has already attained may undermine resolution of *the* fight, by shifting the focus from a couple issue to a personal one. However, in this case, appearance was deceptive. John had been basing his decisions on what Adele needed; and although he was talking about changing that behavior, he had not yet achieved that change.

> Adele: Wait a minute. This is all about me changing. You want my parents out of our lives, and so I have to stop considering them.
>
> John: I never said I wanted your parents out of our lives. I want them out of our decision-making about us. But, yeah, I want you to change. I want you to stop being afraid of your mother.
>
> Adele: I don't think considering what my aging parents want is fear, John. Just because you never see your mother doesn't mean I have to turn into you just to be sane.
>
> John: You're the one bringing up your sanity.

Here comes *the* fight. Let's rejoin them as they resume their conversation about their goal after a break.

> Adele: It feels like you're asking me to change.
>
> John: I am.
>
> Adele: Yeah, but we're dealing with an issue about our relationship. It's not all about how I relate to my parents. I think it's about how we relate to how I relate to my parents.

Her use of metacommunication steered her straight to the point.

John [smiling, and then turning serious]: I think it's both. It's about how you relate to your parents, and then it's about how sick I am of rearranging what I want so you can be comfortable about your parents. And now that I don't want to do that anymore, you're upset with me and we're fighting about them.

Adele [giggling]: It's pretty complicated.

John: Yeah, but you're right that we have to view this as a "we" thing instead of a "you" thing. I think I've done a lot of accommodating. And if we're going to get your parents out of our relationship, so to speak, not our lives, I don't see what more do I can do.

He could stop accommodating. In fact, if they're going to change the way they manage her family of origin, he's going to have to work hard not to fall back into either rescuing Adele or being angry at her about all the times he's already rescued her.

Adele: It's not more; it's different. Maybe you need to let me know what you want, instead of either pushing it aside, like you've done with vacations, or announcing a decision, like about moving.

Great point. Every time John rescued her by protecting her from his feelings, he created a situation in which she didn't know what he wanted her to do. And if one's partner doesn't say otherwise, one usually assumes that either both partners want the same thing or what s/he decides is fine with her/his partner.

John: All right, so you want me to say, "Adele, I don't want to spend Easter with your parents"?

Adele: Not particularly. But if that's how you feel, then yes, I want you to tell me. That way I can deal with it before we've spent Easter with them and you're angry about "accommodating".

John: I don't think you're going to like this.

Adele: Probably not. But if our goal is to make decisions for us as a couple without worrying about my parents' upset, then you've got to stop censoring yourself because you're worried about me being upset.

Here's another great point. When John kept his wishes to himself, he treated Adele the way she treated her mother and sisters: like someone so fragile she would collapse if faced with refusal.

If I were John and Adele, I'd add a second goal, or outcome. In the above examples, John played rescuer, while Adele was rescued. My second goal for Adele and John would be to free themselves from these extreme roles. I view this as a separate goal, because it's possible for them to fall into these roles with any issue, not just Adele's relationship with her mother. I also want to point out that stopping the rescue pattern does not mean ceasing to care or be considerate of the other. It simply means stop assuming one needs to be protected all the time and the other's role is to provide that protection irrespective of her/his own needs or preferences.

Now John and Adele are ready to move on to Step 2: listing options. As they refined their goal in the previous dialogue, they listed one option: John would tell Adele what he wants.

A second and critical option involved Adele doing the same in her relationship with her parents and sisters. This would not be easy for her; she'd been struggling with just that for years. The "geographic solution" worked to a point, but didn't free her from adapting her needs to fit her mother's.

Adele could approach this task by going to therapy or working on it alone. If she decided to work solo, she might use a journal to record what she wants. Then she could review what she wrote with an eye to how much her choices are influenced by how she expects her mother to react. She could also create a picture of what she'd like her life to be like if she and John moved closer to her family. This picture might contain what she would do for herself and how often she would interact with her mother and sisters. Journaling would allow her to play with her ideas and then look at them after she'd had time to think about them. She would need to ask herself how realistic it would be for her to behave the way she wanted without a lot of practice and examination of the obstacles that have been preventing this change all along.

> John: Ok. And you've got to stop censoring yourself because you're worried about your mother.

> Adele: Fair enough. Do we have any other options?

> John: Yeah. We could work on a plan for our lives after Jeff leaves for college.

I like this third option a lot. It's a terrific beginning.

To summarize, Adele and John set a goal of making decisions based on their own needs, rather than anticipating Adele's mother's reaction prior to deciding what works for them as a couple. They also identified three options for action leading to this goal: John cease censoring himself; Adele stop factoring her expectations regarding her mother's reaction into her wishes; and a plan for themselves after Jeff left for college.

With the addition of the second goal I suggested, they would need more options. So, here's an example of how I'd reorganize and elaborate:

1.   Goal 1: Make decisions based on our own needs

Option 1: work on a plan for us after Jeff goes to college—be sure to include how much time we want to spend with our adult children and aging parents

Option 2: set limits on the time we spend with Adele's parents and be sure they understand this is a decision we made together

Option 3: set limits on what Adele will listen to from her mother and sisters and be sure they understand we set these limits together

3.   Goal 2: Free ourselves from the roles of rescuer and rescuee

Option 1: John tells Adele what he wants, rather than censoring himself

Option 2: Adele asks herself what *she* wants and then thinks about how her mother might react

Option 3: Both remain alert to their tendency to slip back into being rescuer and rescuee; tell the other if we think s/he's at it again

Options 2 and 3 for Goal 1 involve setting limits on Adele's mother and sisters, in terms of time spent together and Adele's right to be talked to respectfully by them. I want to reiterate that I am advocating limits, rather than rejection. If Adele and John agreed to spend one holiday a year at her parents' home and to invite her parents to their home once a year, they would be creating time to travel and/or visit their adult children, without removing themselves from her parents' lives. They could begin even more simply, by telling Adele's mother that the grandparents were staying in hotels for Jeff's graduation and offering to make a reservation for her.

Similarly, if Adele told her mother and sisters that she did not want to be told about their disapproval anymore, she would be setting a limit while continuing to speak to them. They might take a dichotomous position—"So, if we say what we think, you won't want to talk to us?"—but as long as Adele remained clear about a third option—talking without criticism—she could remain firm. Hopefully, they would be willing to negotiate with her. Paradoxically, she would be more likely to want to talk to them if she could be confident of a pleasant conversation, free from criticism about her choices.

While the number of options you have is infinite, listing at least three of them liberates you from the either-or dichotomies I want you to avoid. Keep three options a minimum criterion as you work.

Adele and John went on to Step 3 and decided to prioritize their options as follows:

- Goal 2, Options 1 & 2—we'll work separately on our individual issues about asking for what we want
- Goal 2, Option 3—being alert to each other so we stay focused on this goal
- Goal 1, Option 2—we'll begin by Adele or John (their choice) telling her family *we've* decided to ask Jeff's grandparents to stay at hotels for his graduation weekend
- Goal 1, Option 1—plan our future together
- Goal 1, Option 3—Adele will tell her mother and sisters to stop when they're criticizing her
- Goal 1, Option 2—we'll plan to spend some time with the kids, just the five of us (or at most add a boyfriend) this summer and tell Adele's parents together when we next see them about this plan; we'll invite them to our house Labor Day weekend

Adele and John then moved on to enact and assess these options. When they began to plan their future, they undoubtedly needed to become more specific and perhaps fine-tune (assess and rethink their options) before actually making a plan. They needed to practice setting limits on Adele's mother and sisters and avoiding the rescuer/rescuee roles first, so that their plans were not contaminated by these habits.

Since *the* fight manifested itself when they began talking about their future, let's examine an example of their work with Goal 1, Option 1.

> Adele [with a hint of sarcasm]: Ok, John, what are we going to do with the rest of our lives?

> John [laughing]: Well, I feel a bit young to be saying this, but I want to slow down. I've been working for the future as long as I can remember, and it feels like the future is *now*. I'm not ready to retire, but I'm ready to stop going full speed all the time.

Some couples might have gotten stuck here, because John's goal lacked details, and then argued about how to get unstuck. For purposes of exemplifying John and Adele's work, let's assume they didn't.

> Adele: Could you be more specific about what you mean by "slow down"?

> John: What are you, our therapist?

> Adele: I'm just trying to make this conversation work. Though that is probably what she'd ask.

> John: Ok. I want to work 40 hours a week, period. Maybe more at crunch times, but as a rule, no more 9, 10-hour days and a weekend day or two every month. Also, I want to spend less time commuting. If we lived 10 or 15 minutes from where I worked, I'd have an extra hour every day.

> Adele: To do what?

John [shaking his head]: Spend time with my wife. Go visit the kids.

Adele: The kids aren't close enough to visit after work.

Again, many couples would begin fighting at this point, given that Adele completely ignored John's expressed wish to spend more time with her and instead challenged his statement about visiting their children. Again, for purposes of exemplifying the process, let's assume they somehow avoided an argument.

John: Will you stop belittling me? This is all part of slowing down.

Adele: Sorry.

John: Thanks. I'd like to do some woodworking again. Play more tennis. You know, if you want me around awhile, I'm going to have to take some time to get in shape. It'd be great to belong to a tennis club. A gym would be fine, too. We could even go together in the evenings, if you wanted to.

Adele: With all the 20-year-old babes?

John: You're so negative. Is this 'cause I'm talking about living closer to your parents? Are you too angry to want to be around me?

Adele and John were at a crucial point in the discussion. They could easily segue into *the* fight. Although that's what most couples do until *the* fight is resolved, I'm going to bring them back to planning their future, so you can see how important specifics are to success.

Adele: Maybe, but I'd pictured us strolling through our neighborhood after dinner, or maybe power walking with the dog. I really don't want to take my aging body to a gym.

John: Ok, that's negotiable. The bottom line is, I want to have more time to enjoy my life and to be with you and the kids. I know it's late for the kids, but I'll take vacation time to see them and I don't want to be in a situation where I'll suffer at work because of it. I hope whatever it is you decide to do won't interfere with our traveling to see them, either.

John, like most parents, needed to grieve the end of his childrearing years.

Adele went on to talk about her own decision about her future. She was of two minds. Part of her wanted to return to college and study interior design; she'd always been fascinated with color and fabric. Another part of her wanted to open a teashop; she'd talked to a friend about doing it together, which would, of course, mean staying in the city where they and the friend currently lived.

When they arrived at Step 5, assessment, Adele and John realized that they'd talked about their own plans but not about what to do as a couple to enact them. The question of how each could reach her/his goal without impeding the other remained unanswered. They needed to examine how they could work together to create a life they both wanted. And then they needed to do it, so that they could assess the outcome.

John: Ok, Adele. Here's the hard part. How am I going to slow down while you do whatever you decide you want to do?

Adele: I don't know. If I don't open the teashop with Harriet, we'd have more options. I could open one on my own in [Mike's town]. Or, I could go back to school and then do interior decorating wherever we live. It'd be more fun to work with Harriet, but who knows who I might meet after we move.

John: I don't like asking you to give up working with Harriet. How far had you two gotten with your plans?

Adele: In truth, not very far. We'd said that'd be fun. But she's not sure they can afford to invest anything in it, and I haven't thought about what it'd do to our friendship if she worked for me. There are a lot of potential problems.

John: So, it's not like you've been looking at property and here I come and pull the rug out.

Adele: Not at all. Really, my biggest upset is how I'm going to survive living close to my mother and sisters. But, I'm coming around to the idea that I have to change how I am with them anyway. Could you to slow down without moving if I got a real job?

John: Honestly, I don't think so. There's no way my firm would go for it, and going to work in a new place or striking out on my own would be at least as much work as I'm doing now.

Adele: So, it's not just the cost of living here?

John: No. That's part of it, but not the whole thing.

Adele: Have you asked your managing partner?

John: No. It'd be a risk, and I'm not sure I'm willing to take it yet.

Adele: Yeah. OK.

This productive conversation was aimed directly at resolving *the* fight in Adele and John's relationship. If they continue to work together in this vein to plan their future, set limits as a couple on Adele's mother and sisters' behavior, and avoid the rescuer/ rescuee roles; they will probably find that they no longer fall into *the* fight when making plans.

Pete and Shelly: Doing the Best We Know How

We left Shelly feeling hopeless, lonely, and scared about her future with Pete. She confided to a friend that she couldn't remember when they'd been happy, though she knew they had been. She told a friend she felt rejected, misunderstood, and furious that he could let their relationship go.

Shelly: He promised to love me, and he doesn't.

Mary: He loves you in his way. You just don't see it.

Shelly: No, he just wants to get away from me. And it's not about Andrew. He was like that before.

Mary: I think he's grieving.

Shelly: Maybe, but I feel like there's something the matter with me, or he wouldn't be so distant.

Mary: You're being too hard on both of you. Are you looking for an excuse to leave him?

Shelly: I don't know. I'm so confused.

Shelly resonated with the idea of using empathy as a tool. She tried to imagine being Pete, trying to deal with the loss of his father and at the same time feeling betrayed by his wife. Shelly found herself thinking that if the tables were turned, she wasn't sure she could forgive him for having an affair while she was grieving a parent. But she knew that Pete, like his father, took life as it came. She wasn't sure what he thought about when he was alone, but she believed he was healing and that perhaps he used alone time the way she used talking to friends.

Shelly: Pete, I want to be nicer to you about your time alone. Could you help me understand it? Like, what you do?

Pete: Well, you know what I do. I putter in my workshop. I read. I listen to music.

Shelly: No, I mean to work out your feelings.

Pete: I'm not like you, Shelly. I don't think about how I feel all the time.

Shelly: Well, then what do you think about?

Pete: Oh, things.

Shelly [plaintive]: Please, help me understand why you want so much time away from me.

Pete: It's not *about* you, Shelly. I just, I don't feel like talking and be around people.

Shelly: I don't understand. If you're not thinking about it or doing something about it, when will it ever end?

Shelly's empathy broke down here, and her anxiety about her future with Pete emerged.

Pete [angry]: Is that what you're looking for? A date when I'll want to say, "Sure Shelly, make plans for every free second we have from now until the end of time"?

Notice how Pete's reaction changed from explanation to anger.

Shelly [angry]: Oh, cut the sarcasm, Pete. Yeah, I'd like to know when you'd like to rejoin me here in the world of the living.

Pete: Not while you're yelling at me.

Shelly: That's hardly the whole problem.

Pete: You think it's me, and I think you're living in some fantasy of how I used to be.

Shelly: And I think you're depressed.

Here's *the* fight about closeness.

Pete: Well, then go find someone who isn't. I'm sick of hearing about what you think is wrong with me.

And here's *the* new fight about violated trust.

Shelly: That hurt.

Pete: Yeah, well you'd be amazed how I feel about it.

As *the* fight progressed, Shelly lost her ability to use empathy. And empathy only helps when it can be sustained.

At this point, Shelly decided that if things were going to change she would have to change herself, rather than Pete. She'd read enough self-help books to know she couldn't change him, but found herself angry with him for once again making her responsible for their relationship.

Shelly's notebook

Step 1—I'd like Pete to want to spend time with me. We'd get home from work and he'd say, "What do you want to do this evening?" and mean together. We'd go for walks, to movies, and eat with friends. We'd talk about work and politics and having children. We'd exercise together and plan our future.

Step 2—
1.   I could suggest we do something together or talk, but I've done that and it doesn't work

2.   Pete could approach me to do something together or talk, but he won't

3.   I could leave him alone until he comes around, but I'm not sure he ever will

4.   I could tell him I want him to pick a time and something to do and suggest it to me, but he probably wouldn't

5.   I could initiate sex, but I think he's too mad at me and too depressed

[Shelly didn't seem to have any good options, as she accompanied each with a disclaimer. Notice also that Shelly cannot initiate Option 2, so it's not really an option for her.]

Step 3—Option 4 first. Then options 3, 5, and 2.

The following conversation occurred when Shelly attempted Option 4.

Shelly: Pete, you know I'd like to spend more time with you. When I initiate, you always say no. So, I'd like you to pick a time and something for us to do.

Pete: I don't always say no.

They're in trouble already. Pete shifted the conversation to a disagreement about how he reacts when she requests time together. This detour could easily lead them to *the* fight about closeness.

Shelly: I think you do, but that's not the point. Are you willing to ask me to spend time with you?

Pete: This is ridiculous. I spend time with you when I want to, and sometimes when I don't.

Shelly: Then apparently you don't want to because I don't see that we spend any time together.

Pete: Why would I want to when you're like this?

Shelly: I don't know what to do. I can't ask, and you don't want to suggest anything. Any ideas?

Pete: I don't know, Shelly. This whole thing seems to be more of a problem for you than for me.

Metacommunication helped them get back on track, even though they failed to resolve their argument and instead continued *the* fight. Shelly assessed the outcome and decided there wasn't anything else she could think of to do on her own except wait, and waiting hurt.

Relinquishing the job of initiating closeness may be a good idea when one partner has taken sole responsibility, as Shelly has. However, waiting for Pete to ask for closeness left Shelly wondering whether he cared about her, and her hurt thinking he probably didn't increased her frustration and lessened her motivation to live the way they were living. Simultaneously, her concern about delaying having a child at her age increased.

Shelly concluded that she needed to know sooner rather than later whether her relationship with Pete was going to work. So, she approached Pete about going to couple counseling, and he agreed. We'll return to a description of their relationship therapy in Chapter 8.

Serena and Brad: When is enough?

Having given up on identifying *the* fight in their relationship, Serena and Brad began to work on the five steps for resolving it. Please remember that, without awareness of what needs changing, it is virtually impossible to change it. Since Serena and Brad did not identify what they wanted to change, their chances of somehow finding it during the change process diminished significantly.

Once again, they kept separate notebooks.

Serena's notebook

- I'd like us to stay married and raise our child together
- Brad has to decide whether that's good for him, and I guess I do, too
- We need to talk about it until we decide

Brad's notebook

Time limit to decide
Try a separation

Serena initiated the conversation.

Serena: I'd like us to stay married and raise our child together. I think you need to decide whether you agree. And, I think we need to talk about it.

Historically, the commitment problem had been mutual, which Serena ignored.

Brad: I know.

Fortunately, he avoided becoming defensive about whether commitment was an individual or a couple problem, at least for the moment. However, defining a relationship problem as an individual problem won't help resolve *the* fight.

Serena: And?

Brad: I still think we should try another separation. We don't know how we'd feel this time, because of the baby.

Serena [incredulous]: And you have to move out to find out? You can't just figure it out?

Brad [defensive]: I'm not the only one who's moved out, you know.

Serena: Yeah, but that was before Cliff was born.

Brad: Well, I wouldn't want him to think he'd trapped his parents with each other.

Serena [angry]: Grow up, Brad.

Brad [angry]: Hey.

Serena: I don't want him to think his commitments to people don't matter, just because he's not sure he's fulfilled. Do you want to teach him he can always just walk, no consequences?

Brad [reasonable voice tone]: Hey, Serena. We've always agreed that if we weren't better together than apart, we'd split up.

Serena [exasperated]: Brad, you're 40. It's time you knew what you want. It's time to get on with it.

Brad [angry]: I'm sick of you being so self-righteous. Either we're in this together, or I'm out of here.

Serena [quietly]: Ok. My friend Susan and her partner went to a counselor about some stuff, and she said it really helped. Would you go with me if I made an appointment?

Brad [hesitant]: I guess. But I don't see how it'll help me decide whether to split up to go with you.

Serena: Maybe it'd help. And, at this point, anything seems worth a try.

Brad: Well, I'm for that.

For Serena and Brad, questions about commitment are a relationship problem. While each has struggled separately with issues of commitment, the history of these struggles has had an impact on their relationship. Serena and Brad must examine what role their questions about commitment play in their relationship dynamic, as well as in each of their psyches, before they can resolve *the* fight. For example, does the one who doubts the value of the relationship retain power? Or does their history reflect some covert contract about distance regulation that requires adjustment?

I suspect that Serena and Brad have very permeable individual boundaries that leave them unable to tolerate too much closeness and commitment. Thus, when one feels unable to maintain an identity separate from the other, s/he questions the viability of the relationship in order to regain a comfortable distance. When they separate, the distance becomes too great, so they reconcile.

Serena and Brad had not identified boundaries or distance regulation as issues in their relationship. Thus, there was virtually no way for them to recognize these dynamics and the relationship patterns that ensued without help. Additionally, given how entrenched they were in mutual blame, it would have been difficult for them to resolve *the* fight in their relationship, even if they had been able to identify it. In Chapter 8, I'll describe their relationship therapy.

Conclusion

These four couples illustrate the range of possible outcomes, not the percentage of couples for whom any given result occurs. Alan and Samantha and Adele and John successfully resolved *the* fights in their relationships and then got rid of their garbage.

The fight in Serena and Brad's and Pete and Shelly's relationships remain unresolved. We'll revisit them in Chapter 8. You might view their decisions to go to counseling as accomplishments; both couples recognized that they needed to do something about their relationships and discovered they were unable to do it on their own.

Notice that neither of the couples who decided to go to therapy had successfully identified *the* fight in their relationship. This fact is crucial. If you were able to identify yours, there's absolutely no reason why you can't effectively resolve it. However, identifying *the* fight is not a guarantee that you can resolve it yourself. If you are having difficulty, asking for professional guidance may help you resolve *the* fight and eliminate the garbage before you become so frustrated with each other that you give up. I'll address the how-to aspects of finding a relationship counselor or therapist in Chapter 8.

8

When You Need Outside Help and How to Get It

If you're considering consulting a relationship therapist, you've already put some effort into your relationship. I suspect that what you've read and learned as you've attempted the exercises in Chapters 4 and 6 will help speed your work with whomever you choose as your therapist.

Recognizing that you need outside help is, of course, the first step to acquiring it. In this chapter, I'll provide some guidelines for what might lead you to couples' therapy, some information about how to find a couples' therapist once you've decided to look, and a brief description of what you can expect if you go to a couples' therapist.

Recognizing the Need for Outside Help

Any number of paths leads to the conclusion that couple, or relationship therapy might help. Some couples come to therapy proactively, wishing to avoid serious problems arising in the future. Some couples include two emotionally healthy individuals with minimal baggage from their own pasts who get stuck in their relationship dynamics and need a guide to help them discover and enact their options for getting unstuck. Still other couples are mismatched and struggling with whether they can remain together. A fourth group of couples arrive at therapy having spent so many years accumulating garbage that *the* fight is obscured; these couples need help wading through the garbage, finding the issue underlying it, and stopping *the* fight to avoid creating more of it. And, finally, couples come to therapy to stop the repercussions of each individual's psychological difficulties from further harming their relationship.

The four couples we've followed exemplify the variety of ways partners might reach therapy. Alan and Samantha were stuck in a relationship dynamic that resulted in mutual blame until they successfully resolved their fight. Had they been unable to resolve it on their own, they would have fallen into the first category of couples described above.

Adele and John exemplified how an individual issue can turn into a relationship problem. Like Alan and Samantha, they resolved *the* fight working together as a couple on their own.

Pete and Shelly also demonstrated how one partner's psychological difficulties could harm a relationship. Like Adele's concern with her family of origin, John's unresolved grief resulted in a destructive couple dynamic. Shelly fluctuated between attempting to fix Pete and giving up on him and their relationship. As these vacillations multiplied, they became more extreme, until she engaged in an extramarital relationship with Andrew. Even that did not fix Pete, and so Shelly sought therapy. Hopefully, their therapist will work with this dynamic, as well as with Pete's individual issues and the added issue of trust being violated.

Finally, Serena and Brad brought individual problems to their relationship and fell into a relationship dynamic that created so much garbage that they could neither work together nor identify the underlying relationship issues. Their individual difficulties precluded their ability to work together.

How would you know whether your relationship would benefit from outside help? The following eight signs of the possibility that dealing with it on your own isn't working may help you determine whether it's time to seek a relationship therapist. These eight indicators are not intended to be exhaustive. I encourage you to trust your intuition, even if it flies in the face of one of the following clues.

Finding yourself stuck. Sometimes as a couple moves through the process of identifying and then resolving *the* fight, the work bogs down. Couples get stuck because they encounter a metaphorical boulder along the path that they just can't seem to get around.

When your best efforts don't result in forward movement, it's time to do something else. Intuitively, we do more of the same when we encounter difficulty or frustration, but clinical experience suggests doing more of the same produces negligible or even negative results. Similarly, attempting the opposite rarely works, because it's another aspect of the same process that already isn't working. For example, Shelly's increasing efforts to fix Pete didn't work, nor did giving up on him and having an affair. A relationship therapist can help you search for alternative ways to approach the boulder in your path and then guide you around it. Once you're unstuck, you can either continue to use the therapist as a guide or do the remainder of the work on your own.

Two clues that you're stuck involve thinking, I can't do this anymore and frustration about your lack of progress to the point you're unsure you want to continue. Pete and Shelly found themselves stuck, as their notebooks demonstrated. So did Serena and Brad. And there were many points at which the other two couples could easily have become stuck. For example, in Chapter 7 there were a number of times when John and Adele were on the verge of *the* fight and for purposes of illustration I interrupted the dialogue and then resumed as though they hadn't reached a precipice. In reality, they probably would have found themselves in the throes of *the* fight each time. And thus they could have reached the point of thinking, I can't do this anymore or become so frustrated they didn't want to do it anymore.

If you find yourself stuck, metacommunication is a great tool for becoming unstuck. However, if your attempts at metacommunication about being stuck have not resulted in progress, you may need intervention from a third party, i.e., a therapist.

The boulder itself can also be a clue that you need help. If you are stuck and metacommunication has not helped, see whether your boulder appears in one of the remaining seven clues. The more information you take to a therapist, the easier it will be for her/him to help you.

One or both of you cannot show empathy. When one or both partners lacks the capacity for empathy, completing the exercises in Chapters 4 and 6 will probably be difficult, if not impossible. The good news is that adults can learn to be empathetic. This may not be a rapid process, but it can be accomplished with the help of a good therapist. And it is absolutely essential to resolving, perhaps even to identifying *the* fight.

The following excerpt from Serena and Brad's therapy illustrates how empathy can be taught.

Brad: So, that's our history. It'd be better for everyone if I were on my own for a while, so I could decide what I want to do.

Therapist: You think it'd be better for you. I don't hear Serena saying it'd be better for her.

The therapist suspected that, rather than being empathetic, Brad was assuming, or hoping, that Serena shared his feelings.

People who lack empathy often cannot imagine another person feeling differently than they do. It is as though there is no boundary between the person who lacks empathy and others, and the others therefore must see the world just as the person lacking empathy does. They therefore view disagreements as personal affronts or deliberate attempts to frustrate them.

If Brad believed that Serena's insistence that he honor his commitment to her and their son was a conscious attempt to frustrate him, his anger at Serena would become even more intense. Imagine how upset you'd be to learn that your partner was purposefully attempting to upset you. Brad's belief was tantamount to knowing; believing shifted his perspective and left the situation as if he knew. His outlook increased his anger at Serena, turning a disagreement about the context for deciding about the future of their relationship into a battle about how disrespectfully he believed she was treating him.

Brad: But it would. She's not happy when I'm not happy.

While unhappiness may be contagious between partners, the point is Brad's lack of empathy for Serena and a lack of boundary between their points of view.

Therapist: Serena?

Serena: We've been separated too often and it's never helped us decide whether we're right for each other. We just get back together and then the same old questions arise. It doesn't help to separate, and I think especially because of Cliff we have to decide together this time.

Therapist: Brad, tell Serena what you heard her say.

By asking Serena to state her viewpoint, the therapist maintained the focus on the possibility that she didn't see the situation in the same way Brad did and thus began to teach him empathy. She then helped Serena and Brad use the technique of reflective listening to increase their empathy.

Brad: She said she's hanging on. It's nothing new. She's done this before when I've wanted to leave.

Therapist: That may be true, but I don't think that's what she said. Serena, please repeat what you said.

Serena: This time, we have to work out whether we want to be together without separating.

Brad [to therapist]: You want me to repeat that?

Therapist: Yes.

Brad: Ok. She doesn't want me to move out.

Therapist: Serena?

Serena: That's close enough.

Therapist: I think it's very important for the two of you to listen accurately to each other. Serena, I heard you say you think deciding about whether to stay together when you're separated hasn't worked and this time you want to make the decision without separating. Right?

Serena: Yes.

And later,

Therapist: Brad, what do you suppose Serena felt when she said she thought it wasn't a good idea to decide about staying together while separated?

The therapist thus honed in on the emotional component of empathy.

Brad: I don't know. I don't read minds.

Therapist: Of course you don't. But you've known Serena a long time. Based on what you know about her, imagine how she might have felt when she said that.

Because approaching one another empathically involved new behaviors for both Serena and Brad, practice would probably be essential to success. A good therapist will use every opportunity you provide to help you and/or your partner learn and practice empathetic behavior.

You're afraid of your partner. If you're worried about your partner's reaction to the exercises in Chapters 4 and/or 6, you probably need to consult a professional. You may view your partner as too fragile to handle changes in your behavior. Or, you may worry that s/he could become physically or verbally violent.

If you and your partner have any history of relationship violence, I urge you to work with the help of a therapist. Professionals can take the responsibility for prompting the change, thus deflecting some of the consequences onto themselves. They can also help you find the protection you need, should your partner become abusive. You will need a therapist who considers working with abusive couples an area of her or his expertise.

Relationship therapists can assess whether your concerns about your partner's fragility are valid and make suggestions or interventions based upon their conclusions. They can reassure you if your partner is stronger than s/he appears, or work with your partner's fragility if s/he is not.

If your relationship dynamic has evolved around protecting your partner's fragility or protecting yourself from her/his rage, a relationship therapist may be able to help you change this dynamic. John and Adele's relationship evidenced this dynamic. While neither was abusive, they both viewed Adele as fragile and thus

John as needing to protect her from whatever consequences her mother might impose should he insist Adele focus on his needs.

One of you has an emotional problem that interferes with moving forward. Psychological issues can impede success with both relationships and self-help tools. Both Pete and Adele provided good examples of emotional problems impeding forward momentum, with very different outcomes for their relationships.

The symptoms of Pete's grief became indistinguishable from those of depression. Current thought differentiates depression from grief by whether complications arise, including protracted grief, although there is disagreement about how long "uncomplicated bereavement" takes. Pete's prolonged withdrawal was accompanied by a loss of interest in usual activities—he mostly stared into space, rather than working on projects when he was alone—decreased appetite, and increased sleeping. As Shelly suspected, his father's death had forced him to confront his feelings about his father's life, particularly how his father had protected neither himself nor his children from Pete's mother's alcoholism and angry outbursts. Rather than allowing himself to be angry and sad for himself and his father, Pete experienced intolerable guilt for being angry with a dead parent. He subsequently avoided any negative feelings about his father, with the result that he dampened all of his feelings for him. The result was Pete's inability to experience and then move beyond his grief; instead, he got stuck in depression.

Shelly, not being a therapist and being Pete's wife, was unable to help Pete recover. When she attempted to penetrate the wall he'd built around himself, he felt threatened with intolerable feelings of anger at his father and guilt about his anger. He avoided feeling any of this by resisting Shelly, and *the* fight developed.

While Pete and Shelly had always differed in their needs for togetherness and for time with friends, their dissimilarity hadn't previously created such intense negative feelings between them. So, *the* fight about distance regulation developed after Pete's father died and was associated with Pete's unresolved mourning.

Adele also brought issues from her family of origin to her relationship with John. These issues became part of the caretaker-caretakee relationship dynamic that underscored *the* fight between them. John and Adele were able to work through the exercises in Chapters 4 and 6 without a therapist's intervention, in part because they were so open with one another about Adele's issues with her family. However furious they became with one another never impeded their ability to metacommunicate, make their implicit relationship contract explicit, use empathy, question assumptions they'd made about each other, and get unstuck from their disparate goals so they could see and enact their options for resolving *the* fight in their relationship. Had they been unable to succeed on their own, a relationship therapist could have helped Adele acknowledge the impact of her relationship with her mother on their marriage, John acknowledge how he protected Adele at his own expense, and the two of them learn and use these relationship tools.

One or both of you is ambivalent about continuing the relationship. At the beginning of my work with any couple, I always make sure that each partner understands what the other wants for the future of the relationship. Essentially, there are three choices: stay together; separate; or work to decide between the two. Of course there are others, for example, staying together unhappily or staying together and making some or all of the changes that would enhance the relationship. But, if one partner thinks they're there to work on staying together while the other isn't sure, the risks for the first partner are too high. S/he is safer understanding that the goal of determining the future of the relationship is all her/his partner is willing to commit to for the moment.

Shelly's concern about her future with Pete exemplified this reason for seeking outside help. As her attempts to engage Pete failed to bring them closer, Shelly became uncertain whether she wanted to be with him. A therapist could help her sort out her feelings.

If you ran into trouble working through the exercises in Chapter 4 or 6 because one or both of you is uncertain about your relationship's future, finding a relationship therapist who can mediate your interactions as you make this painful decision may be extremely helpful.

So much garbage you can't see the underlying issue(s). Alan and Samantha almost encountered this difficulty. Initially, they were sufficiently angry at one another that they might have described *the* fight as about the other, rather than about their relationship.

Alan: You always want more from me, but never want to give your own time.

Samantha: You're always angry with me and never do anything you don't want to do.

In other words, the problem is your selfishness, which provides no room for resolution and isn't *the* fight.

Not every couple is as fortunate as Alan and Samantha. Many remain entrenched in this garbage as they work to identify *the* fight. If your efforts to identify *the* fight yield confusion, then you may be unable to separate the underlying issue from the garbage that's accumulated in your relationship.

A relationship therapist can help you, as s/he won't be blinded by your negative emotions. Alan and Samantha's argument over the lawn mower in Chapter 4 offers a hypothetical example.

> Therapist: I understand how disappointed you must feel, Samantha, when Alan says he'll do something and then it isn't done in the time frame you expected. But, your anger seems bigger than that, and I wonder what else you're angry about?

With questions like this, a relationship therapist will help you isolate *the* fight from the garbage you encounter every time it begins.

Resolving the *fight didn't diminish the garbage.* Some couples accumulate so much ill will before resolving *the* fight that they continue to feel angry at one another even when they've stopped generating new garbage. If you continue to react to your partner as though you were still having *the* fight, even after it's resolved, you may need to work, with or without a therapist, on getting rid of the garbage.

Resolving *the* fight stops the accumulation of new garbage. However, it does not guarantee that the old garbage will vanish. You can use the techniques recommended in Chapters 4 and 6 to work on the garbage as though your accumulated anger was another issue in *the* fight. You can also seek outside help to get rid of the garbage.

Once again, Alan and Samantha might easily have remained angry at one another about the twelve years that *the* fight had raged, even after they'd resolved it. Samantha might have found herself furious with Alan for his unwillingness to discuss alternatives while the children were infants. And Alan might have fumed about the pressure and anger she'd directed toward him all those years.

A relationship therapist can help you lose the garbage in much the same way s/he would help you resolve *the* fight. S/he would help you identify it, your alternatives for dealing with it, and then facilitate you deciding and enacting what you really want to do about it.

Therapist: Well, you have several options. You're here, so I suspect you don't want to split up over this. Right?

Couple: Right.

Therapist: You can stay together and be angry at each other for the rest of your lives, which I suspect you also don't want to do or you wouldn't be here?

Couple: Right.

Therapist: Or, you can decide you don't want to be angry at each other any more and we can work to diminish your anger. Are there other options you've thought of?

Once you've committed to diminishing the anger, you can begin using techniques, such as asking yourself what the message from your anger might be, to mitigate it. Samantha's anger at Alan might be a message that she's sad about all the years they were angry at each other and all the years she might have been home more with the kids. Then, she would need to grieve the loss of those years and let it go, because continuing to blame him was detrimental to their relationship, which she wanted to continue, and didn't change the past. Or, her anger might be warning her that *the* fight is about to happen again. In that case, she could reassure herself that *the* fight is over and she doesn't need to anticipate its recurrence or attend to the potential to return to *the* fight in order to avoid its recurrence.

Prevention. Sometimes, couples find themselves slipping into the old patterns that generate *the* fight. If this happens, you can repeat the exercises in Chapters 4 and 6. Or, you can consult a relationship therapist. A therapist might help you finish whatever remains unresolved by changing those feelings, thoughts, and behaviors that lead you back into *the* fight.

Other couples want to make sure they don't slip back into old patterns. These couples may choose to consult a relationship therapist proactively. Such preventive work often short-circuits problems in the moment and prevents them from developing later.

Still other couples want to make certain they didn't miss anything as they resolved *the* fight in their relationship and got rid of their garbage. These couples can also use preventive work with a relationship therapist to circumvent future problems.

How to Find a Couples' Therapist

Psychotherapy outcome research has consistently shown that a good "fit" between client and therapist is crucial to success. Although fit is a difficult concept to measure, this finding makes intuitive sense. A therapist who is a good fit for you would be someone you:

- ***Feel comfortable with***;
- ***Can say anything*** to, even things you've never told anyone else;
- ***Trust*** to avoid saying or doing anything that might hurt you;
- ***Trust*** to be confident and calm when you're feeling vulnerable or frightened; and
- ***Believe can help you***, based on what the therapist tells you and, more importantly, on what s/he does.

Asking people who know you to recommend a therapist is a great way to achieve a good fit. Friends are an excellent source, if you're comfortable asking them. So is your primary care physician, but be sure to ask whether s/he knows the therapist and has had good results with other patients s/he referred to this therapist. Your physician may receive short lists of therapists from insurance companies. These may be good therapists, but if your physician doesn't know them then someone who has never met you and can't possibly understand your unique needs has chosen them. And you need to understand whether the referral source knows both you and the therapist.

Relationship therapists differ from individual therapists. While some therapists work with individuals as well as couples, ask whomever you contact to describe their training and experience with couples. Your interests would best be served by someone who understands and has experience working with the dynamics of relationships, as well as the two of partners as individuals.

An initial call to a therapist will accomplish three things. First, you establish whether your schedules fit. Does the therapist have an opening and if so is it at a time that works for both you and your partner?

Second, establish what the fee will be. This includes the therapist's fee and how s/he handles insurance, if you have it. Many plans do not include relationship therapy. If your plan is managed, find out how the therapist handles confidentiality.

Finally, ask the therapist the most important questions you have, the deal-breakers. Ask the therapist to describe her or his approach to couple work. Listen for attention to the dynamics between you. Also listen for the therapist's willingness to explain her/his approach. If the therapist wants to be the expert you don't question, are you comfortable with this attitude?

If there's a special issue, such as abuse or grief, ask whether the therapist works with it. If you're interested in working with someone who will pay attention to you and your partner as individuals, as well as parts of a couple, say so. If you're interested in a therapist who will focus on your current experience, say so. It is always advisable to state clearly what you want. If you're not sure, that's fine also.

In your initial phone call, listen to the therapist's responses. No matter how confident s/he is that s/he can help you, be sure you agree.

Sometimes it's helpful to schedule a session or even two to get acquainted and then decide whether the therapist is right for you. Remember, you are the consumer and while you seek the therapist's expertise, you are the world's best expert on what makes you feel comfortable and safe enough to do the work.

Relationship therapists are usually more directive than individual therapists. I think you need a therapist who is willing to interrupt and direct you for couple work to be effective. S/he may need to stop you from falling into your usual patterns once s/he has identified them. Without the therapist's active participation, the session easily gets out of control and if *the* fight ensues, the therapy can do more harm than good.

That said, it is also important for a therapist to observe directly how a couple fights. I usually allow a couple to argue for a while at least once so I can observe, rather than simply hear their report about how it develops and ensues. You need to feel safe, and so it's also important to feel confident that the therapist will stop the fight before it becomes abusive or otherwise destructive.

Since the therapist is working with you two individuals, the relationship between you, *and* her or his relationship with each of you and with you as a couple, s/he needs to direct the focus of the session to ward off chaos. A couple and family therapist named Carl Whitaker wrote that the therapist must decide on the structure of therapy, while the couple or family decides on the content. You are the arbiter of what you're there to accomplish, though s/he may make professional recommendations based on what you tell her/him and what s/he observes while working with you. S/he'll guide you and structure your work on what you bring to therapy.

To summarize, trust yourself. You will recognize a good fit. And then you will get the best possible therapist for you.

What Will Happen in Couples' Therapy?

Therapists approach relationship therapy from a variety of perspectives. Your therapist will ask about your present distress, its history, and what you'd like to change. S/he will then use her/his theory, or world view, and experience to guide her/his clinical interventions, or work with you.

Although half the couples described in Chapter 3 eventually consulted a therapist; my purpose in choosing these four couples was to illustrate the range of problems, rather than the percentage of couples who buy self-help books and then find they have to go to therapy anyway. To illustrate what might happen in couples' therapy, I'll depict what happened to the two couples who sought it.

Pete and Shelly. As you've seen, Pete and Shelly became stuck in their own perspectives, frustrated with each other, and therefore unable to identify *the* fight in their relationship. During the first session with their therapist, they described the history of their relationship and gave the therapist background information about themselves. The therapist did an informal depression assessment on Pete because she recognized that he was dealing with unresolved issues that preceded his father's death. She then offered him the choice of treating his depression as part of the couple work or seeing someone else for individual treatment. Pete chose the former.

Their therapist was particularly interested in the meaning of Shelly's affair to both of them. She encouraged Pete to verbalize his reactions to it, which, up to this point, he had kept entirely to himself. She asked whether either of them had ever experienced similar feelings and asked them to imagine themselves in those circumstances.

Pete said that at when he was about 8 or 9 there had been a surge of rage from both his parents. He thought it happened just before his father became so silent. He was unsure what had prompted it, but there had been a lot of yelling late at night and his mother had threatened to leave. When asked how he'd felt listening to the yelling and threats, Pete said he couldn't remember. When pressed, he recalled deciding he didn't care, which the therapist reflected as he didn't want to care. When the therapist speculated that many children would have been terrified at the thought of their mother leaving, Pete responded, "I might have been scared. But I don't remember."

Therapist: I wonder where that memory went.

Pete: I don't know. I guess maybe I was relieved. She was already drinking a lot, I think, and I was tired of the yelling.

Therapist: How would your life have changed if she'd left?

Pete: I guess I would have been alone a lot.

When the therapist also speculated that a child might learn to associate yelling with someone important leaving, Pete concurred but once again could not apply that notion to himself.

Therapist: Let's go back to the idea you would have been alone a lot.

Pete: I was already alone a lot anyway.

Therapist: Really?

Pete: Yeah. I didn't have many friends and the ones I had I didn't see after school. And I didn't play sports or anything.

So, I mostly went to my room to do homework and mess around. And stay out of her way, I guess.

Therapist: What would happen when you got in her way?

Pete: Oh, she'd get mad at me. I think she liked to be alone.

Shelly: Oh, come on, Pete. She liked to drink.

Therapist: Let's come back to that. I'd like to focus on Pete right now, Shelly.

Shelly: Ok.

Pete: No, she might be right. She played bridge with her friends in the afternoon and talked on the phone. But when I was around, she'd get mad and accuse me of being under-foot. It was easier to stay out of the way.

Therapist: And safer?

Pete: Yeah, and safer. Do you think I'm hiding now? Staying out of the way? Is that where you're going?

Therapist: It's possible. I'm curious what you think.

As Pete began to consider that he could be safe with Shelly, the therapist worked to be sure that Shelly's anger and hurt at Pete's previous withdrawal didn't threaten any efforts on his part to reach out to her. She also helped them negotiate doing things together which they both enjoyed. To do this, she asked them to take turns suggesting couple activities.

As Pete began to acknowledge his reactions to the important people in his life, he began to talk about his father's life, their re-lationship, and Shelly's affair. The therapist helped him recognize that his anger at Shelly would not drive her away, but rather let her know he loved her. She encouraged Shelly to remain empathetic as she listened to Pete, so that he would experience anger as distinct from driving loved ones away.

At this point, the therapist suggested they consider Shelly's need for distance. Shelly was surprised.

> Therapist: I'm struck by the fact that until Pete's father died, you two had a pretty comfortable balance of closeness and distance.
>
> Shelly: What do you mean?
>
> Therapist: Well, Pete kept the two of you from becoming overwhelmed with closeness and you kept the two of you from drifting apart. Then his father died, and things became too heavy on the distance side. But I think by forcing the issue, your affair may have actually brought you back together.
>
> Shelly: But I always wanted more closeness.
>
> Therapist: And what would you have done if Pete had responded and wanted to spend as much time with you as you wanted him to?
>
> Shelly: It would have been wonderful.
>
> Therapist: How?
>
> Shelly: Well, we would have done everything together: friends, hobbies, raising a family.
>
> Therapist: Sounds like you really don't like to be alone.
>
> Shelly: Oh, no. I hate it. That's one of the things that really attracted me to Pete, how comfortable he was with himself when he was alone.

Here's Shelly's half of the distance regulation issue. She despised being alone, yet chose a man who was comfortable alone.

This suggests some interest in being more like Pete. It also suggests the pitfall of finding that the thing(s) you most admired in your partner at the beginning of the relationship are the things that frustrate you later in the relationship.

The therapist went on to address Shelly's discomfort being alone and suggested ways for her to comfort herself and then enjoy her time with herself. As it turned out, Pete's distance had already helped her develop some of the skills she had so admired in him.

Throughout therapy, their therapist encouraged Pete to express his feelings while remaining empathetic to Shelly's pain. Of course, Pete was also angry about the years she'd blamed him for a problem that also resided in her.

Finally, the therapist helped them move beyond their hurt and anger about the past to explore what they wanted for their relationship in the present, including an amount of distance balanced with closeness that worked for both of them. In the safety of therapy, they also talked about their dreams for the future and discussed having a baby.

At this point, Pete and Shelly began to see their therapist less frequently. The three of them continued to monitor the progress they'd made, and the therapist helped them stay on track. At their final session, they discussed potential pitfalls in the future. Pete and Shelly agreed to call the therapist if they felt themselves slipping back into *the* fight, to avert another crisis.

Serena and Brad. Serena and Brad lacked the self-awareness needed to identify *the* fight in their relationship. I suspect each had difficulty tolerating the concept that s/he contributed to it. It is not unusual to become so furious at one's partner at some point in the relationship that one refuses to acknowledge responsibility for her/his contribution to *the* fight. However, refusing to acknowledge one's part in *the* fight to one's partner is very different from refusing to acknowledge it to oneself, and in Serena and Brad's case I am suggesting the latter. Additionally, since neither Brad nor Serena could provide the other with an empathetic response, any move toward increased self-awareness might have been met with lack of understanding or even scorn. So, even had they had self-awareness, the self-revelation involved in resolving *the* fight would probably have felt unsafe. And thus, their efforts to identify *the* fight in their relationship devolved into mutual blame. And these recriminations deflected their attention from the underlying couple issues.

Therapy could only prove helpful if both Serena and Brad could feel safe enough to approach the problem as a relationship issue. Additionally, both Brad and Serena needed to relinquish their ambivalence about each other and about being in a relationship, irrespective of whether it represented *the* fight or part of their garbage. And both Serena and Brad needed the self-awareness and empathy to tolerate both their own and the other's upset.

Chapter 3 contained excerpts from Serena and Brad's therapy, and I invite you to reread them. Their therapist viewed their problems in terms of commitment and realistic expectations from one another. As he worked to keep Serena and Brad focused on their discomfort with too much closeness, he simultaneously interrupted the angry exchanges between them. He taught them ways to respond empathically to one another and questioned those assumptions they held about relationships that had led them to judge their own as deficient.

However, as their relationship improved, their threats to leave also increased. When the therapist suggested this dynamic might indicate discomfort with closeness, Brad became furious and fired him. After another separation and reconciliation, they tried a woman therapist, hoping she would be less confrontational. However, after a couple of months, Brad deemed her incompetent.

Not surprisingly, Serena and Brad again separated and eventually divorced. But even the finality of divorce didn't end *the* fight. Both were ambivalent about custody, child support, and visitation, and the legal proceedings dragged on for several years. Their attorneys referred them for mediation, and the mediator eventually suggested divorce counseling.

Couples like Brad and Serena, where each partner has her/his own individual issues and resulting ambivalence about relationships and neither evidences empathy, probably need to postpone couple therapy until each has worked individually. However, when partners who have already been separated multiple times present for therapy as a couple, the luxury of time to work on individual issues prior to beginning relationship therapy no longer exists. In these cases, I usually recommend that each works with an individual therapist while we work on couple issues. Ideally, such work would involve close collaboration among the three therapists involved. Sadly, the reality of mental health funding, as well as time demands on couples with young children, often precludes such work.

Conclusion

We have examined the concept of *the* fight in a relationship and nine issues common to many couples for whom a particular fight to express their relationship distress develops. You next worked on a process of identifying *the* fight in your relationship and then resolving it. Finally, we have examined the potential role of relationship therapy in resolving *the* fight, preventing its recurrence, and getting rid of the garbage.

We also observed the lives of four couples, as they proceeded through the tasks presented in this book and as two of them also engaged in therapy. Although all four were not successful, their stories allowed you to see how to most effectively identify and resolve *the* fight in your own relationship, as well as some options when your independent efforts don't work.

As in previous chapters, I encourage you to congratulate yourself, both for your fortitude and commitment to reading this book and for your efforts toward bringing about change in your relationship. The work may be difficult; hopefully the rewards have been great.

References

1. Sapphire-the Uppity Blues Women. (1994). How can I say I miss you? *Old, New, Borrowed & Blue.* Alligator Records.

2. Perls, F. S. (1977). *In and Out of the Garbage Pail.* New York: Bantam Books.

3. Bretherton, I. The origins of attachment theory. John Bowlby and Mary Ainsworth. *Developmental Psychology* (1992), *28,* 759-775.

4. Johnson, S. M. (2004). *The Practice of Emotionally Focused Marital Therapy. Creating connection (2nd ed.).* New York: Brunner/Routledge.

5. Broderick, C. (1988). *Marriage and the Family (3rd ed.).* New York: Prentice Hall

6. Jacobson, N.S. & Margolin, G. (1979). *Marital Therapy. Strategies based on social learning and behavior exchange principals.* New York: Brunner/Mazel.

7. Personal communication, veracity unknown.

8. Minuchin, S. (1974). *Families and Family Therapy. Cambridge MA: Harvard University Press.*

9. Bowen, M. (1985). *Family Therapy in Clinical Practice.* New York: Jason Aronson.

10. Gilligan, C. (1982). *In a Different Voice. Psychological theory and women's development.* Cambridge MA: Harvard University Press.

11. Sager, C. J. (1976). *Marriage Contracts and Couple Therapy.* New York: Brunner/Mazel.

12. Napier, A. Y. & Whitaker, C. A. (1978). *The Family Crucible.* New York: Harper & Row.

13. Tannen, D. (1990). *You Just Don't Understand. Women and men in conversation.* New York: HarperCollins

14. Myers, D. D. (2008). *Why Women Should Rule the World,* New York: Harper Collins.

15. Stosny, S. Lions without a cause. *Psychotherpy Networker,* May/June 2010, pp. 27-53.

16. Luepnitz, D. A. (2002). *Schopenhauer's Porcupines. Intimacy and its dilemmas.* New York: Basic Books.

17. Capra, F. (1991). *The Tao of Physics.* Boston MA: Random House.

18. Mark, K. & Engels, F. (1848). *The Communist Manifesto.* Publisher unknown.

19. Erikson, E. H. (1950). *Childhood and Society.* New York: W. W. Norton & Co.

20. Harris, T. E. & Sherblom, J. C. (2008). *Small Group and Team Communication (4th ed.).* Boston MA: Pearson Education.

www.ingramcontent.com/pod-product-compliance
Lightning Source LLC
Chambersburg PA
CBHW030252290526
45785CB00001B/54